This book is destined to start a new revolution in the financial services industry.

As a leading authority on women and money, it has long been clear to me that women relate to money very differently than men do – and the industry is just beginning to embrace this truth. Adri Miller-Heckman is stepping up to bridge this gap by giving financial advisors a roadmap to serving the female client in a way that truly works for her. In doing so, advisors are discovering a richer, more fulfilling approach to all clients – both male and female.

Adri has artfully combined the strengths of women with the experience and wisdom of men to create a new, refreshing business model for financial advisors. She speaks directly to what advisors need – and what clients want.

This is a must-read for any financial professional looking to create a deeply meaningful and highly profitable advisory practice.

Barbara Stanny
Bestselling author of:
 Prince Charming Isn't Coming
 Overcoming Underearning
 Secrets of Six-Figure Women

The Keys to the Ladies' Room

A *NEW* Business Model for Financial Advisors

Adri Miller-Heckman

authorHOUSE®

AuthorHouse™
1663 Liberty Drive
Bloomington, IN 47403
www.authorhouse.com
Phone: 1-800-839-8640

Published by AuthorHouse   12/17/2012

ISBN: 978-1-4772-9832-9 (sc)
ISBN: 978-1-4772-9831-2 (e)

Library of Congress Control Number: 2012923405

TABLE OF CONTENTS

Introduction: We've Come a Long Way, Baby xi

Section I: **Yin and Yang**

Chapter 1: The New Paradigm 1

Chapter 2: Making the Shift 11

Chapter 3: Your WHY is the Bull's-eye 25

Chapter 4: Going Tribal! 31

Section II: **Building Your Purpose-Driven Practice**

Chapter 5: Tribal Hunting 47

Chapter 6: Your Story 53

Chapter 7: Your Compelling Introduction 69

Chapter 8: A Purpose-Driven Process 99

Chapter 9: Tell Me... Why YOU? 131

Section III: **The Launch**

Chapter 10: Spreading the Word 143

Chapter 11: Drip, Drip, Drip... Getting Your Message Out 147

Chapter 12: You are a Magnet 159

WHAT PEOPLE ARE SAYING ABOUT ADRI...

"In working with Adri, I have gained more clarity, direction and focus to my business than ever before. I continue to generate more referrals and new introductions, and by incorporating Adri's 'Purpose-Driven Wealth Process' with my clients, I now systematically uncover more business opportunities and generate more production. Today I feel so much more confident that I am providing incredible value with less effort. As a result of working with Adri, I attract more prospects and close more business."

~ Katie Morris, CFP

"Before my work with Adri, my creativity in my business was unbounded, but unfocused. People could hear my passion and commitment, but not how I could make a difference in their lives. I just assumed people were getting my message, but my business results showed me I was wrong. Through Adri's program, I now know what to focus on to drive my business forward and connect with people clearly and powerfully. The greatest benefit of all of this has been seeing that I already had all the know-how and the right elements in the business. I just had to get it organized into the most powerful package and statement. That has been gold for me, and has truly jump started my business!"

~ Athena Murphy

"Adri really got me thinking about my purpose. Her questions on how to figure out your purpose were amazing! It helped me refocus on why I am in this business."

~ Jennifer Shields

"Adri really got me thinking about my purpose. Her four questions on how to figure out your purpose were amazing! It helps me to refocus on why I am in this business."

~ Jennifer Meier

"Adri's process took my '30-second commercial' to a whole different level!"

~ Carla Berko

"I was in a place of ambivalence, feeling stuck and unable to move ahead. Adri helped me recognize that it doesn't pay to try to be all things to all people. This was diluting my energy and generating less than stellar results. I am truly impressed with Adri's ability to peel away the layers and get directly to the underlying issues."

~ Liz Murphy, CFP, MBA

"I've learned how to thrive instead of survive as a female in the financial industry. Thank you!"

~ Annie Lynch

ACKNOWLEDGMENTS

My sincerest thanks go out to all the wonderful financial advisors I have had the privilege of coaching over the past 12 years. Your commitment to your own personal development, your desire to provide value, and your courage to break out of the typical industry mold is a constant source of inspiration to me.

INTRODUCTION:

We've Come a Long Way, Baby

John was cold calling commodities, approaching complete strangers, trying to convince them to buy and sell contracts of pork bellies and soybeans. He paid little to no regard to whether these products were suitable for his prospects, even though this was a highly speculative venture. All he needed was a name, address and Social Security number.

Lynn was selling units of a limited partnership, providing eight-year tax shelters for the wealthy. Although the tax benefits were not really what they seemed, the lucrative commissions earned her a big corner office.

Across the hall, Ken was rebuilding his stock and bond practice, struggling to recover from a failed oil-and-gas firm (and the steady flow of lawsuits that followed).

Across town, Gary was advising his clients (mostly elderly retirees) to aggressively trade highly-margined CMOs (collateralized mortgage obligations). All the while, he was profiting from small swings in price – which he was manipulating with the traders.

Leo was taking kickbacks from his largest client, riding a wave of notoriety as a million-dollar producer – until the true nature of his arrangement was revealed and he lost his license.

These stories are not fictional or embellished. I pulled them from my personal history in the financial services industry. The unfortunate truth is they are typical examples of Wall Street ethics in the 1980s.

In hindsight, these activities were clearly inappropriate and unethical, but at the time only a few of them were officially considered illegal. In the 1980s, product was king, the phone was a broker's best friend, and the title *stockbroker* exuded wealth and prestige. This was the era of "smiling and dialing." Training was focused on sell, sell, sell, and overcoming objections was the key to success. Nobody mentioned the clients' needs.

Commissions were high, oversight was minimal and churning was rampant. The industry cultivated a warrior mentality, highly focused on trophies and competition, and incited a culture of competition and greed. Production numbers were posted in common areas, and business was transacted and celebrated over martinis, cigars and other mood-altering party favors.

That is, until the party came to a screeching halt. Tales of unscrupulous behavior in the industry began to emerge through lawsuits, and the public backlash was fierce. This initiated sweeping changes in the industry.

Looking to leave the stained reputation of stockbrokers in the 1980s, the title of Financial Advisor fell into favor. (Of course, at the time it required neither more education nor additional certification.) Advisors shifted toward a planning-based approach to wealth management and suitability became a prominent issue. Profiling also became a central aspect of the work, and advisors began spending more time getting to know their clients before recommending a product or solution.

Those down-and-dirty, over the phone transactions now required more customer information, compliance approval, and far more comprehensive due diligence. While the desire to sell product continued to dominate the business, a more thorough assessment and a computer-generated financial plan now authenticated the recommendation. The industry began to promote a three-appointment process, and managed accounts and "wrap fees" helped slow down the transactional process, thereby reducing conflicts of interest.

While the industry was headed in the right direction, and the new relationship-driven process seemed a more ethical approach to financial services, old habits can be hard to break. Churning continued to threaten industry ethics and the "Good Ol' Boy" network was alive and well.

Management continued to encourage a client-centric process, enforcing the practice through day-to-day scrutiny. As the "wrap fee" concept began to catch on, advisors felt hard-pressed to justify their fees year after year. So, what did industry leaders do? They encouraged advisors to provide a quarterly review to their clients – despite the fact this practice ran counter to the fundamental principles of long-term investing, which downplay the importance of short-term swings in investment value. How else could advisors justify their fees and validate their value?

Investment performance continued to be the yardstick of success until the late 1990s when, with Sandy Weil leading the charge, wire houses and banks began to merge. This provided advisors with a whole new bag of tricks to justify their title and fees. Advisors gained access to a trove of products and services, and they began to encourage their clients to consolidate their assets under one firm and one advisor. With this, the "relationship" approach to financial services was really beginning to take root.

Our current environment

Today's advisor is well aware of and committed to building an ethical, client-centric practice. Most have embraced the fee-based business model, shying away from proprietary investments to avoid conflicts of interest. Service has become the primary objective, and even portfolio management has transitioned from an ad-hoc approach to a more established discipline and process.

Paralleling the medical industry, generalists are being pushed out and teams of specialists are becoming the preferred method for managing the total wealth of an affluent client. While production continues to be a focus, assets under management now drive the business.

Advisors are no longer pushing products; they are looking for ways to present themselves, their integrity and their ability to execute a plan that is perfectly suited to a client's specific needs.

While the focus of the individual advisor has changed dramatically over the past few decades, a number of high-profile scandals have reignited public skepticism of our industry *(thank you very much, Bernie Madoff)*, and this public unease continues to put financial advisors on the defense. Understandably so.

To be honest, the public is right to remain suspicious. The internal compass of the industry as a whole is still spinning wildly, and the small changes we've seen in products and regulations haven't been enough change to appease the concerns of most people.

The industry is ripe for a revolution, and like any great revolution, it has to start in the roots – with the people who are working in and being served by this industry. It's time for a new paradigm, one driven by the voice of the public, the needs of the clients, and the hand of the financial advisor.

Introducing a new paradigm

The growing presence of women in the financial arena, both as advisors and clients, is forcing a shift in the culture of the industry. It had to happen. Our industry was created by men, in service to men, with masculine protocols that feel downright foreign to most women. Yet women are a rapidly growing demographic in the financial services industry. There have never been more female advisors or female clients than there are today.

Statistics show that women are living longer, earning and inheriting sizeable sums, and becoming more engaged in the process of managing their wealth. And it has become crystal clear that women are NOT happy with the status quo in our industry. The old-school approach often undermines and underestimates the intelligence and interest of the female client.

Women are craving – no, *demanding* – a more balanced, holistic approach to finance. This isn't about man vs. woman; it's about yin and yang, like the balance you find in a great marriage where the man and woman recognize, respect and flow with the strengths of the other gender. When women combine their innate gifts with the wisdom of their male counterparts, and integrate their unique strengths as women in the process of money management, the world of finance takes on a very different feel.

Because women tend to be relationship driven, they are more inclined to invest in long-term relationships. Nurturers by nature, they think of their money differently than the numbers-oriented men. And perhaps most importantly, women are usually motivated by a purpose that runs deeper than a paycheck.

When we acknowledge, support and leverage these qualities, the financial-planning process softens and grows more personal. What's more, it gets easier on everyone involved – more profitable, more inspired, and much more attractive.

It's important to note that this gender-balanced way of doing business positions you as the advisor of choice for both men and women. It encourages trust, communicates a sense of ethics, and forms an environment where all of your clients feel well taken care of.

The new paradigm also serves the advisor well, regardless of gender. You will no longer have to "defend" your role as a financial advisor; on the contrary, you will inspire greater confidence by saying less and doing more with a service model that is more personal yet less time intensive. Your relationships with clients will grow stronger, maybe even bordering on friendship, and instead of "prospecting," you will be out engaging in activities with people of similar interests. Your business growth will be fueled by referrals and new introductions, with a stronger foundation of client loyalty that generates more and more raving fans.

In the Keys to the Ladies Room you will begin to understand the influence women will have on your business and future success. By acknowledging women's strengths you will immediately begin to create a more female friendly practice. By implementing a more purpose driven business model you will create an environment that builds new relationships faster, inspires greater loyalty from existing clients, attracts more women, generates more referrals and motivates you for years to come.

The Keys to the Ladies Room is about creating a more Purpose Driven Practice that appeals to all genders.

This is the new paradigm, and if you invest in the process I present in the following pages, it will transform your reality.

SECTION I:

Yin and Yang

CHAPTER 1:

The New Paradigm

If you are still reading, clearly you are searching for something more, something different. Maybe you sense something is missing. I applaud your willingness to explore new ideas and embrace change! In our industry, so steeped in tradition, these are not common qualities.

Let's face the facts: our business was built by men, for men. Every aspect of this business was designed around the strengths of men. Protocol is based on what works for the male advisor and what attracts the male client. From the way we engage clients to the way we advise them, there is a strongly masculine feel pervading the industry.

We first experienced this masculine influence in the training programs, where advisors are taught a linear approach to building a business: prospecting, selling and closing. Historically, most prospecting was done by phone; 80-90 percent of your time was spent smiling and dialing. Detailed phone reports made it easy for managers to monitor activities.

When women entered the sales force, their networking skills (a natural strength) and preference for face-to-face interactions proved difficult to monitor. Managers couldn't measure how much effort or impact was generated each day; there was no report showing how many people these advisors were meeting with. So their efforts were often disparaged. They must be "out getting their nails done," right?

Women were strongly encouraged (and that's putting it lightly) to adhere to the 250-dials-a-day policy, even when their networking was creating better results. How else could they be managed and kept on track? The industry wanted hard numbers!

While achieving financial success is important to all financial advisors, this goal resonates more strongly with men. For many it's their primary motivator, with competition a close second. To leverage these factors, industry managers often post production lists in a central area, complete with quotas, goals, rankings and rewards.

Women don't relate to this culture the same way men do. They respond to the human element – most notably, the desire to nurture and care for others. It's their softer nature, and historically, this set them up for a culture clash with the industry. Its focus on numbers has systematically undermined their sense of purpose, which is so essential to their process and progress.

To compensate for this imbalance, women have learned to conform, adapt and incorporate a more masculine approach to finance. And they've done an admirable job! But no matter how hard they tried, it always made for an awkward fit. What's more, this process of adapting to a heavily masculine industry has caused many women to lose sight of their own natural strengths, strengths that are critical to their desire for success.

For example, in most offices, long hours earn advisors a certain degree of credibility. "He who gets in the earliest and stays the latest is the hardest-working financial advisor." Yet, this directly conflicts with women's innate drive to accomplish more in less time.

So rather than working at peak efficiency for eight hours, women felt compelled to put in longer hours – even if they were unproductive hours that robbed them of the chance to nurture their loved ones. Over time, this imbalance eroded their motivation and desire to succeed.

Even seminars have long reflected the masculine, warrior mentality. For years, attendees focused solely on the features and benefits of the products, rather than the ethics and values of the companies, advisors and clients. "You have a need, I have a solution. Let's shoot it, bag it, and take it home."

Today, the seminar experience is a bit more female friendly. Smaller group events, where participants engage in conversation in a more intimate setting, are fostering stronger relationships and a sense of trust. This smaller environment is ideal for the female client and advisor, and even male advisors are beginning to recognize the value of a softer approach. But I think we can all agree that evolution has not come easily to our industry.

Finding your voice

As an advisor, you developed your skills within a very controlled environment. That highly structured world has dictated your processes, behaviors, even the scripts and language you use. While many of these structures are immovable, there is plenty of room to operate and speak in a way that feels less indoctrinated and more authentic.

That said, it is not easy to craft your own style in an industry that is so dominated by tradition. Shedding these old scripts can be as difficult as escaping that internalized voice of your parents when you speak to your own children.

When I was a new parent, I was determined to incorporate my own "evolved" ideas in raising children. It wasn't that my parents' methods were bad; I just wanted to become a different kind of parent. However, I was surprised to find it incredibly difficult to break free of the scripts I had soaked up as a child. There were times when I sounded *just* like my parents. Their words, even their tone of voice came flowing out of me. It was scary! And the busier I was, the more I reverted back to these ingrained patterns. It was so programmed, it felt instinctual.

To carve my own path, I first had to start by making a firm commitment to myself. Then I had to shift my habits and behaviors to make room for my own unique style of parenting. This required a sincere and concerted effort.

To make purposeful changes to your practice, you will have to make that same conscious effort to drown out the voices of the industry. This process requires a willingness to examine and dismantle traditional industry business-building guidelines, and learn to develop your practice within a different framework – a gender-balanced and purpose-focused paradigm.

Make way for the women

The influence of women, both as advisors and clients, has grown so much that it can no longer be ignored. Statistics indicate that women will soon be controlling the majority of the country's wealth. As of 2012:

- Women comprise 51.4 percent of the U.S. population, yet make or influence 85 percent of all purchasing decisions.

- Women account for $7 trillion in consumer and business spending.

- Women control more than 60 percent of all personal wealth in the U.S.

- Women are starting businesses at twice the rate of men.

Yet *Smart Money* reports that over 70 percent of women feel underserved and dissatisfied with the financial-planning services they receive. So, the more you incorporate a female-friendly style in your practice, the more effective you will be at setting the pace for success in the new paradigm of financial services.

A male advisor once told me, "I treat my women clients exactly the same as my male clients!" Therein lays the problem. While we are all equal, men and women are NOT the same. As we learned in *Men are from Mars, Women are from Venus,* men and women approach life from entirely different directions. While men take a focused, linear approach to wealth, women think of and relate to their wealth more holistically. Psychologist Michael G. Conner writes, "Women tend to be intuitive global thinkers. They consider multiple sources of information and factor in their interconnectedness before making a decision, and can have difficulty separating their personal experience from problems. Men tend to focus on one problem at a time. They take a linear or sequential perspective, and can be prone to minimize and fail to appreciate subtleties that can be crucial to successful solutions." Understanding these fundamental differences is critical to building a female-friendly and purpose-driven practice.

When you ask a client "What are your goals for this money?" you are taking a masculine approach. However, if you ask a female client, "What is the purpose for your money?" you are appealing to her global sensibilities, which often results in more feedback from a woman and a deeper understanding of her needs and desires. While this information provides the advisor with greater insight to make appropriate decisions, it has many other advantages as well. By drawing her deeper into conversation, and recognizing that her style and perspective may be different from her spouse, you are building a foundation of mutual respect and loyalty.

According to author and private wealth specialist Hannah Shaw Grove, "Where competency and results create loyalty in the male client, it is not enough for the women; women factor in the interpersonal and the advisor's communication skills into the equation." So, in a nutshell, if a woman doesn't like and relate well with you, you probably won't get her business (no matter how many degrees and recommendations you have).

Today the industry is shifting, learning to incorporate and cater to the strengths and tendencies of both men and women. *Hallelujah!* This represents a massive breakthrough for female financial advisors and for clients.

In the following chapters, you will learn what it takes to develop a female-friendly financial practice, and establish a process that aligns with and encourages women's natural abilities. It may feel a bit unorthodox… especially for the men. However, it will soon feel much more natural and authentic than the cardboard routine you're running now. *I promise.* Just bear with me, because this shift you're about to make opens the door to a goldmine of opportunity, both personally and professionally.

The woman's way

Women bring a plethora of unique and natural strengths to the world, but we're going to focus now on the particular qualities that support your role as a financial advisor. As you explore these core strengths, you will immediately recognize ways to leverage them in your meetings and interactions with female clients, and gain a level of traction that you never could before. Whether you are a woman, or you are working with women, the following traits are guaranteed to influence your process.

Women are relationship driven

Relationships take time to develop. It's a reciprocal process, with gradually escalating "you show me yours, I'll show you mine" exchanges. It is a two-way process, and learning to accelerate it is truly an art.

When you profile a female client, she needs to learn about you and your life as well. It is not just the product or service you can provide that will secure her business; it's the relationship you develop with her.

Women only do business with people they like. If you want to do business with her, let her get to know you.

Women are made for multitasking

Women are often engaged in more than one task at a time. In prehistoric times, women picked the fruits and vegetables, watched the children and kept an eye out for predators while the men were out hunting. As a result, their abilities evolved in a way that lets them accomplish multiple tasks simultaneously. While today's woman is typically not picking berries or watching for wild animals, she is juggling more roles and tasks than ever before.

Although a woman is designed to multitask, she does require a process in order to be effective. Without processes (structures) in her life, she would never be able to manage all of her responsibilities.

Your understanding of this is critical to the women in your practice because in their eyes, your job is not just selecting the right investments; it's also knowing how to make their lives more efficient and less stressful.

Women crave a process that defines how they should work with you. They will feel far more relaxed and confident when you give them a systematic process for achieving their objectives – and they will feel far more certain that YOU are the person they should be working with.

If you've been in the industry for a while, you have seen that your role has changed dramatically over the years. Gone are the days when you were pitching a single stock or bond. Today, you need to manage multiple aspects of wealth and financial security: investing assets, managing debt, protecting assets and planning legacies. It can be an overwhelming responsibility – unless you develop a well-defined process that addresses these issues in a systematized way.

If this realm of responsibility sometimes seems daunting for you, the advisor, think how it must feel to the client. With the pace and scope of today's world, a well-defined process for managing your clients' needs is absolutely mandatory – it supports the best interests of both the advisor and the client.

Women are driven by a purpose

As nurturers, women have evolved to focus on others: raising children, supporting a husband, caring for aging parents and developing community through service and friendship. All of these roles are based on a desire to improve the lives of others. This deep sense of purpose motivates them each and every day.

While women also have a desire to create and accumulate wealth, this is rarely a primary motivator. ON the other hand, helping women understand what drives and inspires them, and clarifying their underlying purpose for their money, is one of the most effective ways to engage them in the process of managing their money.

In a time when greed seems to be such a dominant motivator in our culture, clients need to know that your interest in them is not just about the income they will generate for you. Many of them assume that you only want their business because of the commissions.

This is why it is SO important for you to be able to speak to people on a deeper level. If you can articulate your purpose – what you truly hope to accomplish with each and every client and WHY this is important to you – You will capture their full attention. When they really "get" what drives you, and realize it's more than just a paycheck, they become more receptive to your advice and less concerned about fees and performance.

Women are masterful communicators

Women tend to be very verbal creatures (as most husbands will gladly attest to). Women are known to speak over 75,000 words a day; men typically range around 25,000. So, in general, women get a lot more practice in communicating – and they get pretty darn proficient at it.

This is why women have an easier time developing relationships. Good communication is a cornerstone to every good relationship, and it's defined by open-ended question, good listening skills and the ability to read non-verbal cues.

In your financial practice, communication is not just about filling out a profile or planning questionnaire; it's about learning who your prospect or client really is, listening to their experience and understanding their situation.

Effective communication is all about relating. If your prospect, client or audience can relate to what you're saying, the relationship moves forward. If you talk over their heads, you alienate them and they drift away. (Most advisors do this far more than they realize.)

The best way to bridge the gap is to adjust your vocabulary, speaking in a way that sounds like your tribal market, not your colleagues. This makes you seem much more relatable and transparent – essential qualities in today's marketplace.

Good communication skills become even more critical when you're meeting with a married couple. Sally Krawcheck, a CEO of Bank of America Merrill Lynch, tells a story about when she and her husband met with their first financial advisor. "This advisor never looked me in the eye, but spoke only to my husband. BIG MISTAKE." Regardless of his experience, skills and qualifications, he would never get their business because he did not know how to communicate with a woman. The sad fact is this is a common mistake.

Women bring many strengths and characteristics to the table, but the four that I have highlighted here are highly influential in their relationships with financial advisors. Advisors should make a concerted effort to improve their own skills within these three areas if they want to attract more clients, increase production and accelerate growth.

As you proceed through the process of developing your Purpose-Driven Practice, you will see how each of these characteristics plays an important role in transforming not just your business message and model, but also how you perform your role as a purpose-driven advisor.

CHAPTER 2:

Making the Shift

You'd have to be living under a rock not to know that the financial industry and the world at large have undergone a dramatic transformation in the last decade – and it's still going through it. From stock broker to wealth advisor, commission-based transactions to fee-based management, the industry has transitioned to a more ethical, client-centric practice. Decisions are no longer based on which products pay the most; we now operate according to what is in the best interests of the client. Advisors are provided with more options and solutions, thereby diminishing conflicts of interest; and clients with greater access to information are more aware of acceptable practice standards, thereby raising the bar for advisors.

While the trajectory of the business is certainly headed in the right direction we still have a long way to go. (Need proof? Check the daily headlines.) Nonetheless, the time is ripe for every financial advisor who aspires to develop a business based on a high level of principles and values.

I encourage you to recognize that, in this pivotal time, you are in a unique position, poised to help bring about tremendous cultural shift in the world of finance. You can be a leader of institutional change, just by rejecting the "Good Ol' Boy" protocol and positioning yourself as a trustworthy advisor and confidant to your clients.

To achieve this, we must start by challenging some of the core concepts our industry was built on; concepts that are especially abhorrent to the female gender.

Historically, business was developed through three core objectives:

1. Prospecting

2. Selling

3. Closing

These three objectives have defined the strategies and daily activities of advisors since Day One – and yet, they are now holding advisors back. These foundational concepts have grown archaic. The tide is shifting from superficial transactions and processes to deeper, richer, more meaningful services that elevate both the client and the advisor.

There are three main ways this transformation is taking place, and they are driving a massive shift in the way business is conducted.

1. **Advisors and clients alike are reconsidering the purpose of the financial services industry, and we're adjusting the paradigm to establish a far more client-friendly process.** This industry isn't just about profits on a page anymore. It's about designing and living the best life possible.

2. **Clients and advisors are both shifting the way they relate to women in the financial world.** The influence of women is growing at a tremendous pace, not only in the number of female advisors but also in the number and magnitude of female clients. Female-friendly processes and practices are becoming increasingly important.

3. **Today, being able to speak about "why" you are in this business is just as important as explaining "what" you do for people.** This aspect of your professional brand attracts more interest, makes you more relatable and improves the listener's receptivity to your message.

If you want to survive in the increasingly competitive marketplace, it's important to understand these changes and adjust your way of doing business accordingly.

To make the shift from an old-school, outdated practice to a modern, engaging, client-friendly practice, work your way through the following chapters. Do the exercises as you go, and by the time you finish this book, you will have written your own blueprint for a powerful practice transformation – one that's both inspired and inspiring designed to attract more women clients.

Starting at Ground Zero: managing your mindset

The most important part of this process is *the way you think about it*. So let's start there, and examine a few of the deeper ruts in the road of popular thinking.

When you think of "prospecting," what comes to mind?

Prospecting, the traditional cornerstone of building new business, often conjures up visions of *Glengarry Glen Ross* or Hollywood's *Wall Street* – manipulative tactics and pushy calls, shady characters working their prospects over, treating people as a means to an end in the game of profit and production.

Cold calling has a long and storied place in our industry. Many people have discovered great new opportunities this way. Even I've developed some fabulous client relationships as a result of it – but I'm convinced it's only because my desire to help was sincere, and everything I said was overlaid with a sense of respect for the prospect.

As a national training officer for Smith Barney, I spent three years listening in on the cold calls made by our new advisors. I would coach them through the call, helping them integrate the canned phrases that were designed to overcome resistance and objections. Teaching them to demonstrate care and interest in the prospect (even when they had none) proved absolutely critical in getting the prospect to stay on the phone.

But some advisors didn't care about how long they could keep a prospect engaged in conversation; they were drumming for quantity. In the movie *The Pursuit of Happiness*, Will Smith played an aspiring financial advisor. While trying to turn an internship into a permanent position, he realized that his most strategic approach was to increase the quantity and speed of his outgoing calls, because the more calls he made, the better his chances of reaching someone who was eager to start investing.

This may have worked in the past, or in a movie… but today, speed and volume do not equate to long-term success.

Mike was a young, up-and-coming advisor, highly motivated to achieve the wealth and prestige of a big producer and clearly destined to succeed. He worked long hours and stayed highly disciplined about making his 200 dials and 50 contacts every day. He was the cold calling king, "Rookie of the Year," and top of the heap come bonus time. He had twice as many clients as most of his peers and his production numbers proved it. Everyone knew Mike was well on his way to becoming a million-dollar producer.

But behind the scenes, his picture-perfect world was cracking. He was growing a bit too fond of alcohol, and his inflated ego set him up for a number of conflicts, both in his marriage and in the office.

But these things didn't bother Mike. Brokerage firms had been courting him, dangling juicy bonuses to lure him over to their side of the street, and he thought he was on top of the world. Eventually, the lucrative offers got to him, and one quiet Friday afternoon, Mike made his move. Little did he know this decision would be the tipping point of his life.

Switching companies cost Mike 50 percent of his clientele. As a relative newbie in the industry, he had no idea this could happen. He was shocked, devastated, and riddled with a sense of rejection and failure.

That's when Mike called me for coaching. Over the course of a few conversations, he realized that he had treated his clients like a number and failed to develop a long-term relationship with them. This, combined with a renewed commitment to live a cleaner, more spiritual life, helped Mike learn from his mistakes and rebuild his practice around ethics, values and a newfound appreciation for his clients.

There are a lot of Mikes in this industry – advisors who built their business on a pile of strangers. It's an unsustainable model, for a couple of reasons.

- The "Do Not Call List" represents the voice of the people – and most people don't want you calling them.

- People do business with people they trust and it's terribly difficult to develop trust through a cold call.

- Today, people crave quality in their professional relationships. If you work with "strangers," they have no loyalty or incentive to stick around.

Yet the industry continues to emphasize cold calling as a primary method for prospecting. The efficiency of this process has declined so much, but the industry stands firm with tradition, anchored in the past.

What it should be doing is uncovering a new approach, one that's aligned with people's desire for relationship-based business.

When you think of "relationship building," what comes to mind?

Relationship building is a slower and much more ethical process than cold calling. Instead of taking a stab in the dark, hoping to hit a profitable target, relationship building is based on reciprocity, an ongoing exchange of information.

If you look at how a relationship develops, you'll see it occurs through common interests and a series of opportunities to engage in conversation. These components nurture a sense of trust, and trust is the cornerstone of any lasting relationship.

So, how can you integrate these concepts into your approach to developing professional relationships? Let's use the dating scene as an example.

Amy, an attractive young woman, is sitting at the local bar, enjoying a glass of wine with her girlfriends. Bob approaches Amy with a smile and says, "Hey baby, can I buy you a drink?" Amy glances up at Bob, rejects his offer, turns her back and resumes the conversation with her friends. Bob makes a few more feeble attempts to get her attention, trying

quips and come-on lines that lack any sincerity or interest in
Amy as a person. Not surprisingly, Bob falls flat.

Sound a bit like the cold-calling process? Let's take another look at this same scenario and see what happens when Bob tries a relationship-driven approach.

Amy, an attractive young woman, is sitting at the local bar, enjoying a glass of wine with her girlfriends. Bob, overhearing their conversation, gently interrupts in the hope of engaging Amy in discussion. "Ladies, I overheard you talking about that movie and I was curious to find out what you thought about it? So many women I know are going to see it... is it a chick flick?"

Bob is now showing interest in the women's opinion about something THEY are interested in.

As the conversation progresses, Bob looks for commonalities that will open the door to further conversation with Amy. By the end of the evening, Bob has learned a few things about Amy and she has had a chance to learn about Bob. If he played his cards right, Bob leaves with Amy's phone number – and over the next few dates, he learns even more about her by asking questions that develop the relationship further.

A Purpose-Driven Practice thrives on opportunities to develop new relationships based on common interests and shared goals.

So instead of prospecting, you're developing supportive relationships; instead of selling, you're inspiring people to protect and grow their wealth; and instead of closing deals, you're motivating people to move forward. Let's dig a little deeper into these perspectives.

When you think of "selling," what comes to mind?

Selling is all about pushing a product to achieve sales and commissions. The emphasis is typically on convincing the prospect to realize this is the product for them. It is often a transaction-based process of soliciting a yes or no answer from a prospect that feels backed into a corner.

I cannot overstate the number of advisors who abhor the idea of selling a product. They typically see selling as manipulative, requiring a variety of tactics to get the client or prospect to agree to the sale. So, it's certainly understandable that most advisors want to avoid this type of approach.

Everyone bristles at the idea of are being "sold to," because they assume (usually correctly) that their true interests are being ignored.

My husband and I went into an appliance store, ready to buy a number of items for our new home. Tony greeted us at the door and asked what we were looking for; he then guided us to the correct department.

While he seemed quite knowledgeable about the products, Tony knew nothing about us. He never asked what was prompting this purchase, what we wanted our product to do, or what we didn't like in our current model. Had he learned more about his customers first, he would have uncovered a wealth of interests, concerns and desires, and been able to provide information that related to our situation.

Instead, he spoke endlessly about his experience, knowledge and his ability to give us the best price. (Just like a lot of advisors I know.) As a result we felt guarded, and we asked more and more questions about the products, trying to determine if he was telling us the truth or just trying to make a sale.

When we turned to leave, he handed us his card and said, "You are now my customer. Call me before you buy anything and I will see if I can beat a competitor's price." It was a nice gesture, but he had never developed a relationship with us – and that was the key to getting our business and referrals.

No one wants to feel like a pushy appliance salesman, but unfortunately, the aversion to acting "sales-y" has stymied the growth and production of most advisors. More often than not, it weakens their ability to guide their clients to take action.

So if you don't want to "sell" your clients on the solutions you offer, how can you apply a guiding hand to their situation?

When you think of "inspiring," what comes to mind?

All the great leaders in the world are highly effective in inspiring others to take action. From political leaders to religious leaders, corporate leaders to cultural leaders, inspiration is the tool of choice because it's so compelling and contagious.

If I asked you to *inspire* your client or prospect to do what is best for them, how would you go about doing that?

Inspiring is a process of sharing thoughts, experiences and stories that intrigue the listener and make them want to learn more. These stories trigger people's beliefs and values, and this creates an open, receptive attitude.

In the new paradigm of business building, inspiring plays a vital role. When you inspire your friends, family, prospects and clients to achieve financial success, they become excited about working with you..

As an advisor, you can inspire others by sharing stories from your life and explaining how your financial decisions helped you avoid a potential crisis. Speaking about the impact of your guidance on other (nameless) clients, and how their lives are better because of these decisions, is another way to inspire your listener. But don't limit yourself to the success stories; be sure to include some of the sad and unsuccessful stories. Discussing the most common mistakes that investors are making inspires people to ask about the strategies you use.

The goal is to helping others see themselves in what you are saying. When they do, they become personally invested in your message.

> *When Tony, the appliance salesman, mentioned the two brands of television that he owns and why he chose them, he finally got our attention. When he told us that he had given his older model (same brand) to his nephew, and it was still running strong after 20 years, we were truly inspired. We wanted to know more about that brand.*

Compelling tales of personal experience make it much, much easier to buy into someone's advice.

When you are busy inspiring others, you rarely have time to talk about yourself, your qualifications, tools, resources or products. This information becomes secondary.

Everyone prefers this approach to a barrage of facts and figures.

When you shift gears and start communicating for the sake of inspiring, you're going to notice a few things right away: opening new accounts will become effortless; referrals will become your primary source of new business; and you will feel much less stressed and far more effective in guiding others.

When you hear, "I closed on the prospect," what comes to mind?

When I hear the term *closing*, the hair on the back of my neck stands up. I find it to be one of the most impersonal, degrading terms associated with the industry. It sounds terminal! It implies a done deal, as if the relationship is over. Granted this may not be accurate, but "closing" terminology really communicates a one-sided approach to the relationship. Closing is about you, the advisor, NOT the prospect or client. The tone of this term feels like strong-arming prospects into signing the documents or writing a check so you can meet your number, tally another one up and calculate your commission.

To put closing in a better light, the process is really about motivating the prospect or client to do what is best for them. It's about helping them make a decision they can feel good about and setting them up for a better future.

When you hear "motivating," what comes to mind?

Will was in training for the US Special Forces, and as most people know, it was a grueling process. Every day of training pushed the candidates to do more than they ever thought they could.

On one particularly tough day, Will was ready to give up. "I can't go any further!" He wanted to ring that bell and surrender.

Sensing Will's defeat, his friend Craig stuck with him, encouraging him to keep going. "Why did you enter this program to begin with?"

"I wanted to serve my country, and to make my wife and son proud."

"That's right! And how proud will they be if you give up now?"

"Not at all," Will admitted.

"Exactly. But how proud will they be if you finish this run, complete this program, and go on to be one of your country's most celebrated warriors? Think of the example will you be setting for your son! This decision will change not only your life, but your family's as well."

Craig used what was important to Will to motivate him to continue. In the end, Will finished the program, and with Craig by his side, he became a Green Beret.

By motivating others, you can help them achieve success far beyond their expectations. As a financial advisor, you can use your knowledge and expertise to motivate your clients to do what is best for their future, encouraging them to see the benefits and value of taking action.

While closing requires an ability to use specific tactics to achieve the end result, motivation requires a clear understanding of the client, recognition of what they want, knowledge of the solution and a view to the benefits of taking action.

The choice is simple: convince or motivate. That's the core difference between the old paradigm and the new one. To support your shift, here are three questions to ask yourself every day:

1. How many new RELATIONSHIPS did I build today, and how did I do it?

2. In what ways did I INSPIRE my clients and prospects to protect and growth their wealth?

3. Who did I MOTIVATE today to make important decisions about their future?

CHAPTER 3:

Your WHY is the Bull's-eye

Peg, a successful advisor and rainmaker for her team, landed an opportunity to make a presentation to a family friend with $25,000,000 to invest following the sale of his business. Peg's partners were equally successful advisors with a multitude of letters following their names. Needless to say, they were thrilled with this new opportunity.

They spent many hours preparing for the meeting, wanting to appear highly professional and capable of managing sizeable wealth. The potential client was interviewing a number of advisors, but this team felt they had an edge on the competition because Peg knew the prospect personally.

Two hours into the meeting, the advisors had gone through their entire proposal, touting the prestige of their firm, their well-defined process for managing wealth, and the value of their service and advice. They felt confident in their recommendations and presentation.

As everything was wrapping up, the prospect said, "I just have one more question: Why should I do business with you?"

This caught the advisors by surprise. Really? Wasn't it already obvious?

Pulling themselves together quickly, they reiterated their years of experience, certifications and extensive training. As they turned to leave, Peg knew they had just lost the business.

When the prospect posed his "$25 million question," the advisors thought he was asking, "What makes you the most qualified?" In truth, he wasn't asking that at all. What he really wanted to know was, "Why should I trust you above all others? Do you really care about me, or is it just my money you want?"

If you were in a similar situation, and a prospect asked you, "Why should I work with you?" what would *you* say? Set the book down now and take a moment to really give this some thought.

Being able to speak about the WHY behind your work is the foundation of a relatable and purpose-driven practice.

When interviewing a financial advisor for my coaching program, I often ask, "If I were an ideal, multimillion-dollar prospect, WHY should I want to do business with you?" They inevitably tell me:

Advisor: "Because I'm honest"

Adri: "You are supposed to be honest."

Advisor: "Because I will put your interests first."

Adri: "I would expect you to put my interest first."

Advisor: "Because of my years of experience, credentials and degrees."

Adri: "Well, that's nice, but there are many advisors with similar if not more degrees."

Advisor: "I work for a great company with many products and tools to offer you."

Adri: "I can find those products and tools in many other firms. So, *why* should I do business with *you*?"

As you consider your answer, you have to eliminate all of the obvious answers. All of the other advisors are already saying those. What will set YOU apart? Take a minute to do a little brainstorming.

_____

_____

_____

As you can see, distinguishing yourself is not as easy as it seems. After all, couldn't a lot of advisors say the same thing that you just wrote down?

Most advisors have lost sight of why they do what they do, why they really care about the client, and why they got into this business to begin with. But the public is craving the WHY. It's what accelerates trust and relationships. It is what allows you to outpace your competitors. Yes, your tools and resources are important; but in most cases, they are a commodity that is now available in abundance. But a strong, satisfying WHY is still very much a rarity.

Before you can speak about the why, you need to <u>investigate</u> the why. You have to dig deep, explore feelings and desires, and recognize what truly drives you. Doing the work to understand your WHY is much more than just coming up with an answer to the $25 million question. By investigating your why, you will also uncover your tribal market (more on that soon). From there, you can begin developing a compelling and authentic message that will intrigue and attract your ideal client. In the process, you will create a script so powerful that every word coming out of your mouth will ring true and align with your actions, marketing and business process.

As a National Training Officer at Smith Barney, I developed a class for financial advisors who had returned to training after successfully completing six months of production. The class was called "Defining Your Business Philosophy." At the beginning of the class, I let every student know that their participation was purely voluntary; no one would be forced to go through the exercise with me unless they volunteered.

"The objective of the exercise is to uncover your personal story. This story will create a new focus for your marketing efforts, greater clarity about your passions, and a tremendous tool to help you generate new clients and referrals."

The first volunteer came up to the front of the room and sat down with me. I asked this advisor, "Who is your target market?" He told me it was business owners.

"Okay, I'm a business owner and you have just completed a presentation to me, trying to convince me to become your client. My final question for you is, "Why should I do business with you?"

The advisor launched into a litany of reasons: "I'm honest and ethical, I work hard..." but none of it really satisfied me.

I kept saying "not good enough" and asking again, "Why do you really care about me?"

The advisor was stumped; he had shared all the typical (safe) answers and was growing frustrated. I continued to push, making the audience uncomfortable, and the advisor's anxiety grew worse.

And then it happened: the advisor cracked. He became quite emotional, telling us, "My parents were business owners and I watched them practically work themselves to death, making sure everyone else was taken care of but neglecting themselves. Then they were unable to sell the business and now they live on Social Security! I swore this would never happen to me or any of my clients."

You could hear a pin drop in that room. The audience was mesmerized, and after a few moments of stunned silence, they started to speak. "Wow! That was really powerful!"

"What made it so powerful?" I asked.

"It was the emotion he showed as he told us about his experience."

"That's right! When we speak about what we do and who we do it for, and we really connect with the WHY we do this work, we can't help but speak from the heart. When people speak from the heart, it's extremely powerful. They get heard. So when it comes to marketing your business, this is the only way to communicate."

When I asked for my next volunteer, every hand went up.

Uncovering your WHY is not an easy process. You must continue to peel the onion, layer by layer, until you get to the root of your purpose. It may take some time, but this is work worth doing – because most advisors never get to the "why." They stay in shallow waters, selling the "what" they do and the "how" they do it, but never diving deep enough to really connect and compel others to do business.

This is one of your main differentiators, the cornerstone of your professional brand, so don't let yourself get off easy. Go dig for it.

CHAPTER 4:

Going Tribal!

If I asked you right now, "Who is your target market?"… what would you say? Don't think, just say it out loud.

Did it come to you quickly? Did you find you had more than one? Were you struggling to commit to a specific segment of the market?

One of the first questions I ask any advisor is, "Who is your target market?" In most cases, they list three different groups of people. They almost always say high net-worth individuals (duh), and then they list certain demographic groups like retirees, business owners and women.

Well, if you have three distinct groups, how targeted are you *really?* Think about it.

When I ask an advisor why they aren't focusing on a specific market, they ALWAYS tell me they are afraid they might miss opportunities. They don't realize that by NOT target marketing, they are erasing great opportunities from their field of vision.

Last year, my husband and I went shopping for a car, but we had really no idea what we wanted. As a result, we wasted an entire weekend, going from dealership to dealership, speaking with multiple salesmen. At the end of the weekend, we had little to show for our efforts. So we took a step back, sat down and listed what we wanted in a car. This simple "targeted" list narrowed our choices to just three vehicles. By the end of the second weekend, we drove our new Nissan Armada off the lot.

Before we went shopping, we had no idea the Nissan Armada even existed. Yet, once we bought one, we noticed several on our short drive home. Over the next week, we saw them everywhere! They were passing us on the road, parked on the street. They had been right in front of us all this time, yet we never even noticed them.

This is why it really pays to zero in on a specific segment of people that you want to serve. When you are focused on a particular niche, you begin to see business opportunities pop up all around you.

The real value of target marketing is in the "opportunity value" ... but I'm going to let you in on a dirty little secret: when it comes to opportunity value, target marketing barely scratches the surface.

Okay, let me be blunt: Target marketing does not work. It's an antiquated process that adds little value.

Now, I know that every coach, trainer and manager professes the powers of target marketing and encourages advisors to select a target market in order to succeed – yet very few advisors really pick this up and run with it. That intrigues me, and I think it points to something important.

Target marketing is too big and too broad – and therefore, too *impersonal* – to be effective. That may seem like a sacrilegious thing to say in an industry that has continuously touted the importance of target marketing. After all, if every book, training and coaching practice emphasizes the importance of target marketing, *how can I say it doesn't work?*

With total conviction.

Let me explain. Let's say I select business owners as my target market. There are SO many kinds of business owners: new start-up owners; long-established owners; owners looking to sell; those with five employees and those with 200; sole proprietors; partnerships… each with a different set of needs, issues and concerns. If I select women as my target market, the same holds true. There are single women, married women, business women and those who have never worked a day in their life; divorced women, widows and single moms. Again, each group has a unique set of issues and concerns. This variety makes it very hard to develop a truly magnetic marketing campaign.

In order to effectively market to your ideal client, you must be able to speak to their *specific* issues and concerns.

It's time to get personal

Most advisors have had some personal experience that helps them relate to their target market – and as it turns out, that's what really matters most. If you can really relate to and connect with the people you want to work with, your marketing efforts will gain traction. Why? Because you understand what matters to them most and you can speak to those issues – not just from your head, but from your heart.

When you can relate to the people you're talking to, something magical happens: you relax, open up and instantly become more authentic. Confidence just oozes out of you. Your eyes light up and your voice takes on a more passionate tone. You become magnetic and compelling. You speak with conviction, and in return, people listen. They *really* listen. And they want to engage with you further, because they think to themselves, "This is my kind of person."

That's the golden ticket right there. People do business with *my kind of people* – because intuitively, we stick with our tribe.

> **Target marketing does not work, but TRIBAL MARKETING works like magic!**

Tribal marketing is all about making a connection with others in your tribe. You are tribal marketing all day long, every day, you just don't know it. Think about the last time you went to a social event where you knew no one. You walked in and scanned the room; perhaps you headed over to the bar to order a drink, and you began talking with the person next to you. It took only 10 seconds to realize this is NOT a member of your tribe. The conversation felt like work and you just had no connection, so you quickly excused yourself and searched out someone else to connect with. You continued to scan the room, looking for visual clues as to who you fit with. (We often spot our tribe before we even speak with them.) You started a conversation with someone else and the next thing you know, two hours have passed and the conversation is still going strong. It was an effortless connection.

Now apply this same phenomenon to your business.

When you are working with a client who is not a member of your tribe, everything feels like work. They question your recommendations, challenge your fees, and even the smallest problems become major issues. (As you read this, isn't there at least one client who comes to mind?)

A non-tribal client causes you to question your value. You think about firing them, but heck, you hate to give up the revenues; so you grin and bear it and muddle along. What most advisors fail to recognize is the detrimental toll this type of relationship takes on their business. The energy required to hang on to this client could be used in so many more positive ways, generating more revenues and even referrals. Non-tribal clients DO NOT give you referrals.

This is such an important point I want you to read it again:

What most advisors fail to recognize is the detrimental toll this type of relationship takes on their business. The energy required to hang on to this client could be used in so many more positive ways, generating more revenues and even referrals. Non-tribal clients DO NOT give you referrals.

A tribal client, on the other hand, energizes your business. You love talking with them; you would do anything for them. Your professional relationship borders on friendship. They trust and respect you, and truly value your advice and recommendations. Everything seems to flow with little effort. When you work with your tribal client, you love what you do and that shines through in every conversation. This inspires referrals.

Making the shift: from target marketing to tribal marketing

I recently worked with a successful team of advisors who wanted help rebranding their practice. They had recently left a large wire house, eager to hang their own shingle as independent advisors. While they had successfully transitioned the business, they were now struggling to move forward.

As part of my on-boarding process, I asked each advisor, "What is your target demographic?" Each advisor listed multiple groups: women, business owners, retired military and 401(k) plans. Therein lay the problem.

When I asked them why they had so many different target markets, they pointed around the office: Joan was a woman; Tom was retired military; and they all had business owners as clients. Given these facts, their multiple target markets made sense, right?

Wrong! Their client selection process lacked the most important component of tribal marketing: emotional connection.

As I worked my way through their welcome kit, I learned a lot more about this team. They were a highly patriotic group and firm believers in free enterprise; they all leaned toward being libertarians. When I questioned them about these beliefs and attitudes, their tone of voice went up and you could feel the passion and conviction in their voices. It was inspiring!

With further probing and intensive coaching, they realized that their real passion was helping their clients become financially independent and totally self-sufficient, never depending on the government to live the life they want.

As we focused on their philosophy, they began to recognize the kind of clients they had attracted: they all shared these same beliefs, whether they were retired military, business owners or women. Almost all of their clients had worked hard, created their own wealth, and were highly committed to shaping their destiny through smart financial planning.

This is a prime example of TRIBAL MARKETING.

A tribal market is not just a demographic group; it's a group of people who share certain perspectives, experiences and beliefs about the world... people who care about the same kinds of things, or simply mirror your style and approach to managing life.

For example, a tribal market can be based on people who are highly disciplined and appreciate structure and accountability. Perhaps they tend to be more organized than most, or share your desire for simplicity.

It might be people you share a religion with, or hobbies, even challenges or priorities.

By zeroing in on the specific traits of your tribe, you can develop a compelling message that speaks directly to your ideal client. Eventually, you can revise your business model, making sure that everything you do in your practice reflects these attitudes and philosophies, challenges and personal style. Soon, your tribe will begin to gravitate to you.

If this is so effective, why isn't everyone doing it?

Selecting a target market is much easier than identifying your tribe. Target marketing is like a multiple choice question. Discovering your tribal market takes more internal work, introspection and self-reflection. Then you must summon the courage to embrace your tribe and incorporate its concerns into your practice and marketing strategy. For many people, this is enough to set their nerves on edge.

Here's why: this industry has encouraged you to lose your individuality and adopt a stoic, cut-and-dried image. It gave you guidelines, regulations, even a specialized language (hoping to make you seem smarter, yet often speaking over the heads of your prospects and clients).

When you turn away from this hardline protocol, and you start to incorporate more personal, emotionally-charged language, it can make you feel a bit naked. You may feel vulnerable to rejection by clients or ridiculed by your peers. Trust me, I know. I hear it from nearly every person I coach.

But, here's the interesting thing: every time one of my clients take the plunge and shares their new tribal message, they come back to me with the most amazing results.

"They actually listened to what I had to say!"

"Adri, it worked! After I shared my story at a networking event, two different people came up to me afterwards. This never happened before!"

"When I shared my message, they immediately gave me a referral."

"Adri, using my new message, I revised my website bio after our last coaching call. Within a week, I received a call from a qualified prospect who was ready to do business. She told me she had been searching for an advisor, reading bio after bio, and when she came to mine, she just loved it. She said, 'Your message was so much more personal, it really resonated with me.'"

After experiencing such a positive response to their tribal marketing strategy, all of these advisors became more determined to embrace this new approach, fueling their desire to become more authentic and differentiate themselves from the competition.

In today's marketplace, you differentiate or you die. Financial advisors are constantly looking for ways to differentiate themselves, but as long as you stick to the protocol and vocabulary of the industry, your marketing activities will generate minimal results and you will NEVER stand out.

Jordan is a perfect example of how tribal marketing can transform your business – and more.

Jordan Goes Tribal

When Jordan signed on for coaching, his business was stagnating. He had developed a base of wonderful clients, but he knew he needed to grow and add more clients to his practice. While he was a member of a successful team of three, he was the lowest producer and hesitated to speak up in their meetings. When he did speak up, he felt ignored. His confidence was at an all-time low and he hesitated to make any effort to attract more clients.

After just one coaching call, I began to see who Jordan really was. It didn't take long to realize his faith was front and center in his life. He wasn't one of those preachy types, but it quickly became clear that this was his focus and priority. His tribe was obvious. The question was: would he be strong enough to embrace it?

I asked Jordan to evaluate his top 20 clients. He shared his results with me, talking about their jobs, status in life, gender and how they came to him, but he couldn't see any strong patterns.

"Jordan," I asked, "how many of your clients share your faith in God?" He paused for a moment and then said with a shrug, "Pretty much all of them."

"Well, what does that tell you?"

"That people of faith are my tribe?"

"YES!"

While he was pleased to know he had a tribe, the thought of putting his faith front and center in his practice made him very nervous. It just felt so… personal.

Over time and with a lot of support, he eventually developed a faith-based marketing system – and his transformation was nothing less than amazing. He started the transition simply by changing the phrase "I am a financial advisor" to "I run a faith-based financial practice." This *raised a few eyebrows, but when people asked him for more information, he would tell them, "Most of my clients are faith-based professionals who strive to be good stewards of their wealth."*

His new message generated more interest in what he does, but the biggest impact of his new message occurred at a much deeper level. "Adri, I can't tell you how much you have changed my career. I used to hate coming to work, but now I LOVE it. I am so much more confident and happy, and I am getting more referrals, just by being more transparent about who I am."

Tribal marketing is not just a business concept; it's a way of life. When you focus on your tribal market, your business becomes a reflection of you and your lifestyle. Here's another example.

Dan: A Man in Motion

With just two years under his belt, Dan came to me looking for more focus in his practice. He taught a financial-planning class for an adult educational program, which had been a good source of new business, but it had brought him a motley assortment of clients. He knew he could be doing so much better but he felt like he was all over the map. He just didn't know where or how to focus his efforts.

In the process of learning about Dan, his passion for outdoor sports really stood out. He biked, hiked, kayaked and participated in all kinds of outdoor events, and was passionate about sharing his love of outdoor activities with others. When I probed his client list, almost all of them shared his passion for outdoor activities. They were avid runners, bikers and outdoor enthusiasts. So we began to rebrand his practice around this, starting with a new tagline: "Taking on Retirement with a Vengeance!"

Since rebranding his practice, Dan has become more optimistic and energized. He now hosts events featuring athletes and retirees who have accomplished impressive feats. He even promotes community runs and bike races through his website and drip e-mails. He feels totally in his element, and his confidence and enthusiasm are truly contagious. Not only is he feeling much more in the flow, but the referrals are flowing too.

We all have a tribe. Your tribe might be as evident as your faith or hobbies, or it may be something less obvious like your philosophy, principles, or stage of life.

Allison was a strong woman, determined to succeed and proud of her role as the breadwinner of her family. She had built a successful practice as a financial advisor and was ready to rebrand and focus her energies on the women's market – but which segment?

Thinking of her mother, she first set her sights on widows. But it didn't take long to realize that widows were not Alison's tribe. She just didn't have the patience to work with women who needed more time and energy. She gravitated to women who were dynamic, busy and decisive – many of her own traits – and when we determined that her tribe was Dynamic Women Driven to Succeed in Business and Life, she really came to life.

Regardless of what tribe you belong to, the impact of focusing on it will generate powerful results: more energy, passion and enthusiasm for what you do, and more interest and referrals from prospective clients.

So, what's holding you back?

While most advisors are eager to uncover their tribal market and embrace this marketing strategy, the moment their tribal market is revealed, their anxiety rises and they express concern in two areas:

1. Recognizing that not all of their clients fit their tribal market, they get concerned that their new message and focus may alienate existing clients and cause some of them to leave. **What really happens:** they end up generating more referrals.

2. They fear they will miss out on business opportunities, especially when speaking with those who are NOT in their tribal market. **What really happens:** the opposite occurs. By being specific about who they work best with, they attract more business than ever before.

As an advisor, it's important to recognize that everyone you meet is one of three kinds of people:

1. Your client

2. A qualified prospect

3. A potential marketing agent

Every one of these people needs to hear you talk about your tribal market. Your client needs to know how to describe you and what you do so they can send you more referrals. A qualified prospect wants to hear your message and know more about your intriguing practice. And those who are not destined to be your client can still be inspired to refer business to you – as long as they find your message compelling.

Mr. Solomon was definitely not my tribal market. He was a man who invested all his money with Vanguard, the no-load haven, yet he referred three women to me – and eventually, he too became my client.

I met him through a cold call, and I introduced myself as a financial advisor with Smith Barney who was passionate about working with the Wise Women in Newport Beach. While it was immediately evident that he was not a member of my tribal market, what I had to say intrigued him enough to stay on the phone and continue speaking with me. I shared my story about my mother, validating my commitment to women, and told him about my events, designed to help women become more engaged with their finances. I ended the call by inviting him to one of my money-manager luncheons, which was designed for both men and women. That was the beginning of a long-term, highly profitable relationship.

If I had tried to prospect Mr. Solomon instead of remaining focused on my mission and passion, do you think I ever would have gotten his business? NO! I would have blended in with all the other financial advisors who were cold calling him, trying to lure him away from the no-load world of investing. I had taken a totally different tack, diffused his defense mechanisms and engaged him in a lively discussion.

When you don't have a clear, focused and consistent message, you behave like a chameleon, changing your appearance in order to blend in. Do you hear that?! You are BLENDING IN – which means few people will ever remember what you do or who you like to work with. **This is the main reason you don't generate the number of referrals you want.**

Mr. Solomon not only remembered what I did but he sent me three qualified women, all of whom became my clients. Eventually, he too became a loyal client and raving fan.

Going forward...

As of today, you must focus solely on the kind of client that you WANT to attract, and the kind of practice you want to create. Like Kevin Costner said in the movie *Field of Dreams:* "If you build it, they will come."

Costner played Ray, a farmer who was inspired to build a baseball field in the middle of a corn field. Everyone thought he was nuts, and he too had moments of doubt, but he knew this was what he was meant to do. He went against everything that was logical and reasonable, until eventually he was only supported by his wife and one other character. Once the field was finished, the players came – and so did the tourists who would eventually keep his dream alive.

That same phenomenon can happen to you. In my days of building my practice, the wise women of Newport Beach became my singular focus, and everything I did was designed to help these women. My events were about helping them become more comfortable and engaged, and even my prospecting calls were scripted to emphasize why women needed more financial help. As a result, my whole practice was built by referrals. It worked for me, and it will work for you too.

The following chapters with help you stimulate growth and increase your confidence step by step. You'll find the inspiration, guidance and clarity to defy tradition, step out in a new direction, and build the kind of practice that attracts your ideal client.

SECTION II:

Building Your Purpose-Driven Practice

CHAPTER 5:

Tribal Hunting

Going forward, everything you do and create will speak directly to your tribal market – so if you haven't selected and committed to one yet, now is the time.

While some financial advisors find this to be an easy process, it can be a challenge for others. Often it's a fear of commitment that stops them in their tracks. They're always thinking that there must be a better tribal market out there.

> I assure you, the benefits of identifying and committing to a tribe far outweigh any potential limitations.

There are a number of ways to uncover your ideal tribal market, but the best place to start is to look for patterns: patterns in your business, patterns in your life history, and patterns in your personality. These patterns create a powerful "ah-ha!" feeling of recognition when your tribe comes into focus.

More often than not, advisors come to realize that their tribal market was right there in front of them all along, they just never saw it. But that's not always the case. Your tribal market may not always be what it first appears to be. As you begin your search, you may find a logical tribal market early on, but don't end your search just yet.

It's not uncommon to uncover more than one potential tribal market that seems appropriate. It's important to investigate several potential avenues before making a final decision. The key is determining which tribal market makes the most sense, feels most fulfilling, and best serves your bottom line.

4 Key Ways to Discover Your Tribal Market

Most financial advisors find their tribe by sifting through four areas of their life, each of which provides a different perspective on your likes and dislikes, patterns and history.

YOU

In my coaching practice I typically start looking for clues within the personality of the advisor. Learning about their hobbies, interests, passions, even idiosyncrasies can provide a sneak peek as to who that advisor is best suited to work with.

Robin was in her fifth year as a financial advisor, yet her production numbers failed to reflect her experience and she was on the verge of being let go. It was a final warning from her firm that prompted her to get the coaching she needed.

As I got to know Robin, I started to notice her desire for structure – and an underlying lack of structure in her business. She was extremely goal driven and liked having a step-by-step process, so it quickly became clear that for Robin to succeed, she would need a well-defined process, a systematized service model, and a more defined structure for prospecting in order to achieve her goals.

Structure, numbers and a systematized process were vital to Robin's success, and a significant clue to her potential growth and tribal market. As we began looking for patterns in her existing book of business, I asked her to describe her favorite and least favorite clients. She did not enjoy working with widows or women who tended to take a long time making a decision; their indecisiveness drove her nuts. On the other hand, her favorite client was an engineering type because she found them easy to work with, and they appreciated her value and advice.

I then asked Robin to list her top 20 clients and look for patterns, e.g. jobs, ages, where the client came from, and any other points of similarity. She discovered that five of her top 20 clients were engineers – and that most of them had been referred to her. BINGO! Soon we had identified Robin's tribal market as "detail-oriented individuals who want a structured process with ongoing accountability."

Within a year of doing this process, Robin had doubled her production. By the end of the second year, her upward trajectory foretold a fantastic future in the industry.

With a well-defined process for helping her goal-oriented clients, she was far more effective in her prospecting efforts and she opened the door to a consistent stream of referrals. And, it's certainly worth mentioning that she took more vacation time than ever before and still generated record production.

Your Book of Business

Identifying patterns based on careers, age, and status can be very valuable. While Robin's patterns pointed straight to her tribal market, this is not true for everyone. In many cases, the pattern in their book validates something else entirely.

When I first met Tom, he was an industry rock star with just a few years under his belt. He was achieving all his goals and had been deemed a success by his firm. When Tom pursued coaching, it wasn't to fix his business – it was to accelerate his rate of success.

As I got to know Tom, it was a bit difficult to find the patterns in his personality so we studied his book of business. After reviewing his clientele, we still struggled to find a pattern. His clients had one thing in common: money and a need for investments, but there was no other connection between Tom and his clients.

Over time, with some deep digging, I was able to help Tom identify his ideal client and tribal market, but Tom was resistant to sticking with the program. While I was confident we had identified his tribal market and message, I was not so confident in his commitment to our plan. Tom wasn't focused on his tribe; he was focused on money.

Two years later Tom called me, wanting to start up coaching again. A lot had happened since we had last worked together. Tom had struggled with alcoholism, which fueled constant conflicts with his firm. So, he accepted an offer to move his practice to a new firm. The signing bonus certainly made life comfortable (albeit temporarily), but Tom was in for a rude awakening: less than 50 percent of his clients moved with him.

That's when Tom got it. He had spent years accepting any client with assets and a pulse, but he had neglected to develop any kind of relationship with them. He had little in common with them anyway, since most were not part of his tribal market.

His move to a new firm, plus an alcohol-fueled crisis, had forced Tom to reassess his whole life. In the process, he developed a new passion for his business and he was finally ready to rebuild his business with purpose.

I share Tom's story for two reasons:

1. Your book of business is NOT always an indicator of who you should be focusing on. Many financial advisors have inherited books of business, and while the money and potential revenue is good, it can derail your focus if you have little in common with your clients.

2. Tom's story shows the tremendous impact your tribal market can have on your business. A tribal client is loyal to the core. They are more apt to assign all their assets to you, and they become long-term raving fans, generating a stream of qualified referrals. Because Tom had no client consistency or tribal market, and because he resisted the process of developing one, he received none of the benefits that come with a Purpose-Driven Practice.

I am pleased to say that Tom has found new success in both his business and personal life. He used his experience dealing with a personal crisis to fuel his passion and desire to help his clients live a full and financially secure life. In the process, Tom won my respect and admiration for his ability, determination and the discipline it took to change his life.

Your Experience

In the 1980s and 1990s, most new hires in the industry were young adults, just out of college with no real experience or network. Today, many financial advisors enter the business after a career in another field. While a previous career may not always point to your ideal tribal market, it often gives you the insider knowledge, experience and understanding of core issues and concerns of people in that field, which can be a potent combination when prospecting for new business.

Again, it's not your experience alone that will determine your tribal market; it's who you really care about helping. This can often be uncovered simply by writing your story. (More on that in the next chapter.)

Your Story

Everyone has a story – and yours may be a great way to discover your tribal market. Not only does your story highlight who your ideal client could be, but it also doubles as a powerful marketing tool, because for many people, their personal history inspired them to become a financial advisor.

Your story is more than just a tool to unveil your tribal market; it will become one of the most valuable components of your marketing and compelling message. (That's why I devoted a whole chapter to helping you write your story. It's coming up next!)

CHAPTER 6:

Your Story

Developing your personal story can create a clear window into your ideal tribal market. The beauty of this process is that not only will you end up identifying your tribal market, but you will also create a unique, authentic story that can be shared in a multitude of venues, helping you inspire others to ask for more information about what you do.

The objective of your story is to share with the listener what motivated you to become a financial advisor. In sharing this, you will divulge a little bit about who you are as a person, creating a stronger, more personal connection with the listener. In addition, your story will help the listener recognize that you are motivated to help your clients, not just make a paycheck. And lastly, your story will define for the listener what you truly hope to accomplish for your clients, which goes way beyond just investing their money.

This one story will inspire more interest in your services, create a foundation of trust, and clarify your purpose – all in a magnetic way, pulling your ideal prospect closer and closer to becoming your client.

For most advisors, their story stems from one of the following four scenarios:

1. A childhood experience

2. Your experiences as an adult

3. Experiences of a loved one (i.e. friend or family member)

4. Your experiences as a financial advisor

The one you choose depends solely on you and the experiences that made a lasting impression on you. Some people may draw from more than one experience, but only YOU can determine which story, which experience, delivers the emotionally-charged images that your ideal clients will resonate with.

My own personal story stems from my experience as a child watching my mother struggle to understand the investment world; this had a profound impact on me. Yet, I also went through a divorce and had to face the heavy reality of making ends meet as a newly-single mother. While both experiences were important and memorable, the one with my mother made a larger impression, inspiring me to help other women become more engaged in their financial affairs. I could easily have chosen divorced women as my tribal market; it would have been easy to make that connection, but it just didn't inspire me as much as my experience with my mom.

Everyone has a story, but it may take some serious excavating to unearth it. Some of you may already be thinking about your story, while others may be struggling to dig up a story that has meaning. For many people, the emotions associated with a powerful experience can be so uncomfortable that you distanced yourself from that memory. Now may be the time to resurrect that experience and put it to work for you.

In the following pages, you'll read some examples of well-crafted personal stories that were designed to attract members of a specific tribal market. As you read, feel for the flow of the story. After each one, I will break it down to help you grasp the strategies and recognize how to make your own story concise yet impactful. Let's start with my story, which centers on a childhood experience.

> *When I was young, my father managed all the investments for our family. He wanted my mother to become more involved in the process, but when she tried, he made her feel stupid. Just because she couldn't understand the concepts of yield or PE ratios, he felt she was incapable of learning – and the worst part was, she believed him. I knew my mother was smart; she was a college graduate who managed a household of six kids. There was no reason she couldn't understand investments, but my father made her involvement too painful. As a result, when I became a financial advisor, I made a commitment to focus the majority of my time, energy and practice on creating an environment where women could learn about investing, have fun, and become more confident in making smart financial decisions with less stress and worry.*

As you read this story, you will recognize three components:

1. What happened?

2. What was the result?

3. What was the impact? How did this affect me?

What happened: *When I was young, my father managed all the investments for our family. He wanted my mother to become more involved in the process, but when she did he made her feel stupid.*

The result: *Just because she couldn't understand the concepts of yield or PE ratios, he felt she was incapable of learning – and the worst part was, she believed him. I knew my mother was smart; she was a college graduate who* managed a household of six kids. There was no reason she couldn't understand investments, but my father made her involvement too painful.

The impact: As a result, when I became a financial advisor, I made a commitment to focus the majority of my time, energy and practice on creating an environment where women could learn about investing, have fun, and become more confident in making smart financial decisions with less stress and worry.

As you craft your story, it is important to keep it short and compelling. Most people tend to share way too much information, giving too many unnecessary details and sprinkling in lots of umms and ahhhs. Reread my story and pay particular attention to the specific information I included. Which words and phrases illustrated the story and left an impression? What details would my target market relate to?

Start by writing out your full story, then go back and eliminate the details that aren't really necessary. Or, you can highlight sections that make an impact, and then look for the details that don't add value to the story.

Don't play it safe. Include words that indicate how you feel or felt, and use everyday vocabulary to help you relate to your listener. As you develop your story, get crystal clear on the most important words, phrases and sentences that resonate with your tribal market.

Let's look at another story, this time an adult experience.

> I will never forget the day I went to visit my grandfather in a nursing home – but it's a day I wish I could forget. I knew my grandfather didn't have a lot of money, just his farm, but I didn't realize how bad things were until I saw the state-run nursing home where he would spend the rest of his days. It was such a depressing place. After his death, I learned that his farm was worth nearly a million dollars! My parents, who

had minimal financial knowledge, never thought to borrow against the farm to provide for my grandfather. If they had met with a financial advisor, they would have learned how to leverage the farm to provide a better life for my grandfather, instead of leaving him destitute. That's when I decided to become a financial advisor, specializing in helping elderly people use their assets to live the life of their choosing. Each and every one of my clients are a lot like my grandfather, and I do everything I can to help them generate the income they need to maintain their quality of life, and live and die with dignity.

What happened: *I will never forget the day I went to visit my grandfather in a nursing home – but it's a day I wish I could forget. I knew my grandfather didn't have a lot of money, just his farm, but I didn't realize how bad things were until I saw the state-run nursing home where he would spend the rest of his days. It was such a depressing place. After his death, I learned that his farm was worth nearly a million dollars!*

The result: *My parents, who had minimal financial knowledge, never thought to borrow against the farm to provide for my grandfather. If they had met with a financial advisor, they would have learned how to leverage the farm to provide a better life for my grandfather, instead of leaving him destitute.*

The impact: *That's when I decided to become a financial advisor, specializing in helping elderly people use their assets to live the life of their choosing. Each and every one of my clients are a lot like my grandfather, and I do everything I can to help them generate the income they need to maintain their quality of life, and live and die with dignity.*

As you read this story, what stands out? Go through it and highlight the statements, words or phrases that made a strong impression. Notice that each paragraph only has two or three sentences, so it's important to make each one a high-impact statement.

Ready for the next example? This one is built around the experiences of a loved one.

> *I watched my closest friend borrow $500 and build one of the biggest window and door companies in all of Arizona. He lived a great life in a beautiful home, and he took fabulous vacations. His life was set – until the market turned and his company went bankrupt. While my friend knew how to build and create wealth, he never planned for the future; he assumed his business would always provide for him. My friend had to sell his big home, and today he owes hundreds of thousands of dollars to the bank. He even had to pull his kids out of private school, just to make ends meet. When I became a financial advisor, I decided to focus all my efforts on helping smart, successful business owners like my friend put a plan in place that would provide for their future, protect their assets, and create a source of income that isn't solely dependent on the success of their business.*

What happened: *I watched my closest friend borrow $500 and build one of the biggest window and door companies in all of Arizona. He lived a great life in a beautiful home, and he took fabulous vacations. His life was set – until the market turned and his companies went bankrupt. While my friend knew how to build and create wealth, he never planned for the future; he assumed his business would always provide for him.*

The result: *My friend had to sell his big home, and today he owes hundreds of thousands to the bank. He even had to pull his kids out of college, just to make ends meet.*

The impact: *When I became a financial advisor, I decided to focus all my efforts on helping smart, successful business owners like my friend put a plan in place that would provide for their future, protect their assets, and create a source of income that isn't solely dependent on the success of their business.*

Now it's your turn: write your story

Step 1: Journal your story

The first step is to decide which experience will become the foundation to your story, and then write it out in full as if you were writing in a journal. Don't worry about grammar or structure; just write in free flow, pulling as much as you can from memory. At this stage, feel free to add in as many details as you want. Be sure to incorporate how this experience was impacting you, how it made you feel, and why it was a concern. This is all valuable information that will help you hone in on the most important points.

Step 2: Craft the highlights

Review your story and highlight the words and phrases that stand out. Think of it like this: if others were reading this story, and they only had time to read the highlights, what would you want them to be sure to read?

> **EXAMPLE:** <u>When I was young,</u> we lived in a big house. There were six kids and <u>my mom managed the household while my dad worked as a lawyer. My dad did all of the investing,</u> working with our financial advisor to pick stocks. Dad kept telling Mom she needed to be involved <u>and he pushed her to learn more about investing</u>. I remember watching them review their statements, and <u>when my mom couldn't understand what six percent yield meant,</u> he would get frustrated, almost angry. I could see my mom shutting down; <u>he made her feel stupid and incapable of learning,</u> just because she couldn't learn it his way.

Step 3: Edit your draft

Focusing on the highlighted information, begin editing and condensing the content. Sort it into the following sections:

What happened?

_____

_____

_____

What was the result?

_____

_____

_____

What was the impact?

_____

_____

_____

Step 4: Share it

Once you've honed your story down to its juiciest, most meaningful components, it's time to start "market testing" it. Share your story with people who will give you objective feedback. Start with friends, family members and/or other financial advisors. Watch their reactions, ask for feedback, and write their comments down for further consideration. You will know you have hit the mark when their eyes open wider and their face shows some reaction, not just from the details of your story but **because they understand WHY you do what you do.**

Your mission

As you craft your story, you not only develop a great way to market your practice, but you also develop your mission statement. The last section of your story, how you were impacted, tells the listener what you are really trying to accomplish – that's your mission.

In my story, the last section reads:

> *As a result, when I became a financial advisor, I made a commitment to focus a majority of my time, energy and practice on creating an environment where women could learn about investing, have fun, and become more confident in making smart financial decisions with less stress and worry.*

This last paragraph reflects my mission, drawing on the core message of my story.

> **My mission:** *To create an environment where women can learn about investing while having fun and becoming more confident in making smart financial decisions, with less stress and worry.*

In the story about the grandfather, the last section reads:

> *That's when I decided to become a financial advisor and specialize in helping the elderly use their assets to live the life*

of their choosing. Each and every one of my clients are a lot like my grandfather, and I do everything I can to help them generate the income they need to maintain the quality of their lives, and to live and die with dignity.

Mission: *To treat every one of my clients like they were my grandparents, doing everything I can to help them generate the income they need to maintain their quality of life and have the ability to live and die with dignity.*

In the story about the business owner, the last section reads:

When I became a financial Advisor I decided to focus all my efforts on helping smart successful business owners like my friend put a plan in place that would provide for their future, protect their assets and create a source of income not solely dependent on the success of their business.

Mission: *To help smart, successful business owners put a plan in place that will provide for their future, protect their assets, and create a source of income that's not solely dependent on the success of their business.*

In developing your authentic story, you have:

1. **Uncovered your ideal tribal market,** giving you more focus and direction with your business.

2. **Developed a compelling story** that promotes your business and intrigues others to want to learn more about you and your business.

3. **Clarified your mission statement,** a critical tool that can be used in marketing, posted in your office, and shared with both clients and prospects.

What a great example of multitasking!

So, now what?

Now that you have this great story, how do you put it to work for you? The very first thing you must do is MEMORIZE IT. *Trust me on this.* If you don't, one of two things will happen:

1. You just won't put it to use; or

2. It will come out as a long-winded, rambling story with too many umms and ahhs, losing its impact in the process. It just won't have that WOW effect that you're looking for.

This is your story, your words, your feelings, but it's not written in the "financial professional" language that we have become accustomed to in our industry. Therefore, in a professional setting, it may not feel natural. As you develop additional marketing pieces for your practice, you will find yourself carefully scrutinizing every word and phrase, tweaking things to make them just right so they send your message in a way that your tribal market can relate to. Memorizing your story is part of that process.

Now let's explore some very effective ways to use your story to make a strong impression.

Networking: It doesn't matter whether your market is business owners or widows, affluent families or executives; you can always find opportunities to weave your story into a conversation.

Depending on the specific audience, you may choose to mention only a portion of the story. For example:

You know, my mom was the same way. "When I was young..."

You might change the end to be briefer, saying something like, "It was this experience with my mom that inspired my career." This invites people to ask for more information: "So, what do you do?" This is your invitation to promote your services.

Seminars and Events: True stories are powerful ways to engage the audience and prepare them for the upcoming presentation. By opening your presentation with a story, you not only engage the participants with something that is true and relevant, but it also gives you the opportunity to confirm exactly what you do and who you do it for. Your audience will warm up to you when they hear it.

If you use your story at the beginning of the presentation, you should always refer back to the story at the end of the presentation. The story can emphasize the mistakes or challenges your tribal market may face, so the end is a great time to say what you do with your clients so they never experience the same consequences as the person in your story. This brings the discussion full circle and leaves people with a sense of satisfaction.

Client Meetings: As you develop your Purpose-Driven Practice, it's important to share your new brand and structure with existing clients. They have the greatest potential for becoming your raving fans, but they must be inspired by your new mission and message in order to initiate more referrals. In your meetings with clients, don't hide the fact that you have been working hard to improve your practice.

"Mr. and Mrs. Smith, over the past six months, I have been spending a lot of time evaluating my business and looking for ways that I can provide more value for clients like you.

What I found was quite interesting. I realized that most of my clients are retired, and that I love to work with those clients most. I realized that I do my best work for retired couples like you. In fact, as I thought about this further, I recognized it was my own experience with my parents that really set me on this path." (Now share your story.)

This adds a more personal feeling to an otherwise professional meeting, and your clients will leave the meeting with a better understanding of you who you work for, why you care about them, and what you hope to accomplish with every client. **This is the kind of information that inspires referrals.** In fact, chances are good that as they head home from meeting with you, your clients will be thinking of friends and family members who are retired or nearing retirement and should be working with YOU.

Prospect Meetings: A meeting with a prospect should always be 75 percent about them. But at the point when you have gathered all the information you need, it's your turn to help the prospect get to know you – and more importantly, understand why they should do business with you. This is the time to launch into your story. If you are meeting with prospects from your tribal market, they will automatically relate to what you are saying. Instead of spending 30 minutes telling the prospect about the tools, resources and qualifications you bring to the table, your story will help you leapfrog ahead, creating a foundation of trust and a personal connection. Until they trust YOU, the products are secondary. Remember: trust is the rare commodity.

Your presentation may go something like this:

"Mr. and Mrs. Smith, I've really enjoyed learning more about you, your situation and what you hope to accomplish. I believe we would do very well working together and I look forward to the opportunity; but first, let me tell you a little

about why I got into this business to begin with." (Start your story.)

Your Website: You can use your story on your website in a multitude of ways. Some advisors put it right on the home page in support of their brand. People are more apt to read a short, well-written, autobiographical story before they read a stodgy, boring home page that formally describes how qualified you are. Other advisors place their story on the About page, with the bio. Either placement works well.

This story will say more about you than your work experience and credentials ever will. Regardless of where you place it, your story must be told in as many ways as possible. Eventually, your clients will know your story by heart and then be able to share it with others – which is precisely what we're aiming for.

Drip E-mails: I'm going to assume that you are sending consistent drip e-mails, twice a month to all of your clients and prospects (and I'm going to ignore the reality that many of you are NOT). Use this method to make sure that everyone in your database learns your story. A short story is a great drip e-mail and very effective in engaging the reader. You could start such an e-mail like this:

> *Last week, I met with a woman who had just lost her husband. She was anxious, unsure of what to do, and still reeling from the loss of her husband. Seeing her anxiety, I was reminded of why I got into this business in the first place – and I wanted to share this story with you today, because it really means a lot to me.* (Insert your story here.)

However you choose to do it, get your story out there in a multitude of ways and venues. Speak it, write it, e-mail it, share it… but first, make sure you refine it and MEMORIZE it.

Centers of Influence: With a COI, your story validates the fact that you are truly committed to helping a certain group of people. At the same time, it helps the COI scan through their clients and easily identify the right people to refer. As you explain your tribal market in a memorable way, they develop a mental filter that they then apply to not only existing but future contacts as well.

As you can see, your story has the potential to become the centerpiece of all your marketing efforts. The more you tell it, the more it becomes an integral part of your brand – the way people know you as a professional.

CHAPTER 7:

Your Compelling Introduction

Every time I start coaching a new client, I ask, "What do you do?" Ninety-nine percent of the time, they stumble around and start apologizing, almost as if they are embarrassed to say, "I'm a financial advisor."

You must be able to describe what you do in a meaningful way, with clarity and distinction. The goal is to intrigue people when you introduce who you are and what you do.

Before we go any further, let's make one thing crystal clear: this chapter is NOT about creating an "elevator script." Far from it! The purpose of an elevator script is to help you differentiate yourself by using some packaged phrases to describe what you do. The problem with most elevator scripts is that they feel so contrived, financial advisors never use them.

Most financial advisors give a mini dissertation about what they do, typically boring the listener (who is silently regretting they ever asked). Or, if asked for more information, they stumble around – then later feel bad that they didn't do a better job of explaining themselves.

That said, I think it's safe to say that we all understand the value of a clear and compelling message that differentiates them from the competition. Truth be told, but most advisors have yet to determine the best way to describe their purpose and value.

This chapter will help you solve that problem by walking you through the steps to create your compelling introductory script.

Blending in with your crowd

This script is strategically designed to feel natural and authentic, and consistently inspire further interest. It's not about educating the listener; it's about dropping little nuggets of information to intrigue them. Well, to intrigue the "right" people, that is. If you develop a compelling script, and your listener isn't compelled to ask for more information, chances are they aren't a good fit for your practice. So, a great script does double duty: it attracts your ideal prospects, and it weeds out those who aren't worth pursuing. Talk about a time saver!

For those who are an ideal prospect, your introductory script is a verbal arsenal, breaking down the barriers of inertia and lighting a spark of interest, leaving the listener anxious to learn more and eager to schedule some time with you.

Like a personal story, your introductory script must be very focused and defined, zeroing in on a specific tribal market. The most effective scripts speak directly to your tribal market and their specific concerns, desires and challenges.

It should also reflect their vocabulary. This is *really* important.

As a financial advisor, you will find yourself gravitating to what YOU think they need and want, and you'll tend to speak in financial industry lingo. For example, when asked what their prospect wants, advisors will often say, "They want a financial plan." Now, how many couples lie in bed at night and say, "Honey, we need a financial plan…"? They don't. They might say, "Where is our income going to come from?" Or, "Will we be able to retire when we planned?" Or maybe, "How can we rebuild our savings after getting the kids through college?" Truly understanding what they are thinking, what they are concerned about, and being able to articulate that in their language is essential.

So make a note: going forward, you are not to use words like "diversification" or "asset allocation;" these words have been so overused that their meaning and value to the average listener has long since washed away. "Peace of mind" is out too; along with "review and monitor." How many couples say, "I wish my advisor would review and monitor my portfolio"…? I challenge you to find even one.

As you develop your script, keep asking yourself: *Does my tribal market actually use these words?* If not, your introductory script won't land the way you want it to.

The key is to get inside the mind of your tribal market, look at everything through their eyes and speak to them in their language; this is how you make an immediate connection.

How to create a compelling introductory script

As you begin the process of developing your script, take it one step at a time. If one area becomes a challenge, move on and come back to it later. Creativity can't be forced, so beware of overthinking the process and trying to force your mind to perform. This process requires you to get in the zone, think outside the box and brainstorm without fear. Have fun with this process; let yourself get a little silly and outrageous. You can always trim it back later if need be… or, you just might fall in love with what comes out.

There are four key components to your introductory script. Each component has the ability to work independently, so this provides you with tremendous ammunition when you are face-to-face with a potential prospect. Or, the four components can be used sequentially, unveiling a powerful and memorable introduction to your practice.

Component #1: "I am a..."

The first component of your introductory script is your title – but more often than not, it will be the last piece you create. The purpose of this component is to mention what you do in a way that compels the listener to ask, "What's that?"

When you say you are a financial advisor, does anyone ask, "What's that?" No! Because they already have an idea of what a financial advisor is and does. (Unfortunately, that idea is rarely accurate and it often comes with a side of negative connotations.) Therefore, you need to state what you do in a way that reflects both what you deliver and what your tribal market wants to hear.

For example, if you specialize in working with business owners and entrepreneurs, you may call yourself "an entrepreneurial wealth advisor." This title alone will inspire further interest.

As an advisor focusing on the wealthy women in Newport Beach, I would tell people: "I specialize in wise women and wealth." This was intriguing enough to invite questions, and it was synergistic with the rest of my message.

I worked with a multimillion-dollar team from New Jersey that rebranded themselves as "family wealth advisors." Not only did they focus on managing family wealth, but they were an actual family themselves.

I worked with another team that focused all their efforts on helping Baby Boomers use retirement as a way of fulfilling their bucket lists. So, when asked what they do, they would say, "We manage Boomers and bucket lists." This might sound silly or trite, but it really worked for this team of advisors.

Remember: all you want this part of your script to do is inspire your listeners to say, "What's that?" – thereby inviting you to share more about your work.

Component #2: Describe your tribe

The second part of a compelling introductory script describes the kind of clients you want to attract. Just two, maybe three sentences long, this section describes and compliments your tribal market, and mentions the challenges they commonly experience. This is critical to attracting both clients and referrals; everyone must be crystal clear about the kind of person you work best with.

Let's look at an example:

Wise Women and Wealth

Most of my clients are wise women of Newport Beach who have recently become responsible for managing their money on their own. While they are very bright women, they often lack the knowledge and confidence they need to make smart financial decisions. As a result, they often experience unnecessary stress and anxiety when it comes to their money.

A few things to highlight before we move on:

ALWAYS start with *"Most of my clients...."* This is important because it leaves the door open to others. In my previous story of prospecting with Mr. Solomon, by sharing that "most of my clients are women," I left the door open for him to become a client as well. I didn't say *all of my clients* or *I only work with...* I said MOST of my clients. These simple distinctions can make all the difference between appearing inclusive and welcoming, or exclusionary.

In the first line, I described these women in a complementary way ("wise women"). Then I got more detailed: "...who have recently become solely responsible for managing their money on their own." If you are talking to a member of your tribal market, their ears will definitely perk up; if they are not in your tribal market, they will automatically begin thinking about women they know who have recently become single, which is exactly what you want.

Next, you compliment them again, but also mention the challenges they may be facing: "While they are very bright women, they often lack the knowledge and confidence they need to make smart financial decisions." If you are talking to your tribal market, they now recognize that you understand what they are feeling and experiencing. If they are not your tribal market, again, they are listening and relating this conversation to someone they know.

Here is another important point to remember: If I am talking to a powerhouse executive and I tell him I'm a financial advisor, his defenses will go up and he will automatically assume that everything I say is self-promotion, geared to entice him to become my client. He knows this because he is constantly pursued and prospected by just about every financial advisor in the area. So, instead of acting like a chameleon and changing my story to focus on him (which typically goes nowhere), I share my unique and compelling introduction. This diffuses his defense mechanisms, allowing him to engage in conversation with me. In fact, there is a good chance that while we are talking, he is thinking of his sister, his wife, his daughters, maybe even a colleague that he can refer to me. Because he does not feel personally prospected, he will be more interested in what I have to say. This might compel him to ask, "Do you only work with women?" Voilà! There's a new opportunity with a highly influential prospect.

Component #3: The needs

The next part of a compelling introductory script is all about your clients' needs, issues and concerns. To assemble this component, you must identify the three most common issues facing your tribal market, and then state them in the language that your market uses.

Each one of these needs should represent one aspect of what you do for people. In most cases:

- The first issue represents the need for financial planning;

- The second issue often suggests the need for investment management;

- And the third issue highlights the additional value you bring to your clients.

All of these issues are aspects of your business, but you are repackaging and renaming them in order to develop your brand.

Other coaching programs would tell you to consult with an advisory group, a select group of clients that will feed you the insights and information you need to connect with your tribe. This can be a useful strategy, but don't hesitate to trust that you already know the main issues you need to address. Chances are you just haven't spent enough time thinking about your tribe yet. So take some time to brainstorm now.

**What are the three most common or pressing
issues that my tribal market faces?**

1._____

2._____

3._____

Let's go back to the *Wise Women and Wealth* example to see how these three components fit together.

"What do you do?"

I manage wise women and wealth.

"What do you mean by that?"

Most of my clients are wise women of Newport Beach who have recently become responsible for managing their money on their own. While they are very bright women, they often lack the knowledge and confidence they need to make smart financial decisions.

And you know what's interesting? It doesn't matter how these women became single; they usually come to me with the same three concerns.

"What are those?"

1. *Will I have to go on a budget?*

2. *How can I make sure I never become a bag lady?*

3. *Will I become a burden on my children?*

Can you see how a specific set of women would be very intrigued by this introduction?

You may have noticed a transition piece to link components #2 and #3:

And you know what's interesting? It doesn't matter how these women became single; they usually come to me with the same three concerns.

This little bridge often prompts the listener to ask, "What are those?" This is an invitation to share more about your target market, further describing the type of people you hope to attract.

Notice that the three issues are stated very simply and concisely. Again, you are not trying to educate the listener, just to entice them with just enough information that they start to crave more. By mentioning the most common issues and needs, you're prompting the listener to ask, "So what do you do for them?"

By this point, you have connected with your tribal market; and you have clearly expressed an understanding of their concerns and experiences. This established a sense of trust and credibility. Now, they are eager to learn what you actually do for your tribal market.

This is the perfect set up, so what you say next must be clear and concise.

Component #4: Solutions

When the time comes to describe your solutions, don't try to recreate the wheel – just rebrand it, so what you do makes more sense and becomes more attractive to your tribal market.

In presenting your solutions, it's important to refer back to the three core issues that you identified earlier. These are the issues that are prominent in the prospects' minds and will attract the interest of the listener. Most of what you say should address these needs.

Using the wise women of Newport Beach example, the top three issues were:

1. Will I have to go on a budget?

2. How can I make sure I never become a bag lady?

3. Will I become a burden on my children?

Again, the first issue highlights a need for financial planning; the second issue addresses investment management; and the third issue showcases the additional value you bring to your clients.

Your task is to develop the verbiage to describe your solutions to these problems in a way that is memorable, inspires further interest and reflects your tribal market. This is what branding is all about. So, let's go back to the example and take it a step further.

Solution #1

If my tribal market is women who are suddenly single, and their first concern is about budgeting, chances are the first thing a prospect will be interested in is how much income she will be generating. With that in mind, when you state what you do, you need a magnetic description for your solution to this concern. Instead of saying, *"I will provide her with a financial plan,"* which is about as interesting as wallpaper paste, you can repackage it to say something more along the lines of, *"I create her Personal Income Plan."* Simple, right? All I did was incorporate a few words that reflected this tribal market's particular concerns.

Solution #2

Now for the second concern: "How can I be sure I never become a bag lady?"

Instead of stating, "I will invest her money," or "I provide a managed money platform," you can customize the solution by branding it. For example, you might say, *"I incorporate my Safe Money Strategy."* Chances are the words "safe" resonates with a woman who is afraid of running out of money. This creates a much stronger connection than providing a generic term that really says nothing to the listener.

Solution #3

The final issue should highlight the additional value you deliver. Most advisors say something like, "I then review and monitor the plan and portfolio," but can you imagine how many advisors must be saying that? Just about all of them! What if you changed your phraseology to something more interesting, like, *"Lastly, I provide an ongoing series of Women & Wealth events designed to educate, engage and build confidence in my female clients."* Instead of just saying, "I educate my clients" (*yawn*), you state the value of your events and describe how they will help your tribal market.

Once you craft some powerful wording to describe your solutions, it's important to give each solution a brand name or title. For instance:

- *Personal Income Plan*

- *Safe Money Strategy*

- *Women & Wealth Events*

This positions you to develop your professional brand and presence in the community – an advisor of choice.

Pulling it all together!

Now that we've covered each component, let's pull it all together and bring your introductory script to life. Here's how it goes:

Prospect: *"So Mr. /Ms. Advisor, what do you do?"*

Advisor: *I specialize in Wise Women and Wealth.*

Prospect: *"What do you mean by that?"*

Advisor: *Well, most of my clients are wise women of Newport Beach who have recently become responsible for managing their money on their own. While they are very bright women, they often lack the knowledge and confidence they need to make smart financial decisions. As a result, they experience unnecessary stress and anxiety when it comes to their money.*

(Advisor pauses.)

And you know what's interesting? It doesn't matter how they became single; they typically come to me with the same three concerns!

Prospect: *"What are those?"*

Advisor:

1. *Will I have to go on a budget?*

2. *How can I make sure I never become a bag lady?*

3. *Will I become a burden on my children?*

Prospect: *"So what do you do for them?"*

Advisor:

1. *I create a Personal Income Plan.*

2. *I incorporate my Safe Money Strategy.*

3. *And I provide and ongoing series of Women &
   Wealth Events designed to educate, engage and
   build confidence in my female clients.*

As you can see, each section is prompted by a question. If they don't ask a leading question, odds are they aren't interested in your services.

More than the sum of its parts

While this introductory script was originally designed to work sequentially, each section can be used independently. Imagine yourself at a social event and perhaps the conversation shifts to someone's mother who just became a widow. This would be a perfect time to share the three core issues that single women experience. It might sound something like this:

Gosh, I'm really sorry to hear about your mom. It's interesting, most of my clients are women who have become suddenly single as well, and in most cases, their three most pressing concerns are:

1. *Do I have to go on a budget?*

2. *Will I end up a bag lady?*

3. *Will I end up a burden on my children?*

What has been your mother's biggest concern?

Don't assume you have to use the script in its entirety, especially when networking and socializing. Again, all you are doing is dropping nuggets to tempt your ideal clients. You will have plenty of opportunities to share your complete compelling introduction – at your next event, in a one-on-one presentation with a prospect, talking with centers of influence, talking with organizations about their employees, the list is endless. There are a plethora of opportunities where it is completely appropriate to share your entire introductory script.

Real-life examples

Now, I will provide you with a number of real-life introductory scripts that were created by advisors just like you. Although many advisors find themselves feeling protective of their message, hesitating to share it with other advisors for fear of seeing their idea get stolen, these advisors have learned that even if someone tried to copy their intro script, it just wouldn't work for them – because if it's not authentic, it won't make an impact on listeners. The key to a powerful introductory script is YOU and the way you speak to your unique tribal market. By copying someone else's work, you lose the authenticity that comes through when you create it yourself.

As you review the following examples, feel the flow of information, and the words and phrases that stand out to you. Get a sense of the impression the advisor is trying to make and the way they accomplish that.

A Faith-Based Practice

"So Christina, what do you do?"

I run a faith-based financial practice.

"What's that?"

Most of my clients are families of faith; they have accumulated substantial assets and are compelled to be good stewards of their wealth. For most, this means ensuring their lifestyle, enhancing their family's sense of safety, and contributing to their community. But the pace of life often causes them to lose focus. They want to work with an advisor who shares their beliefs and will continue to hold them accountable to their stewardship goals. (Pause.) What's interesting is that it doesn't matter who refers them to us; they all come to us with the same three concerns!

"What are those?"

1. *How can I maintain my lifestyle and not outlive my money?*

2. *How can I use my wealth to enrich my life and those of others?*

3. *Who can we work with that will support and encourage our priorities?*

"So what do you do for them?"

Together, we:

- *Design their Lifestyle Priority Plan,*

- *Incorporate a Balanced Investment Strategy,*

- *And I provide a Values-Based Educational Program.*

···

Passionate Wealth

"So Dan, what do you do?"

I manage passionate wealth.

"What do you mean by that?"

Most of my clients are successful professionals and passionate outdoor enthusiasts. They have worked hard and saved well, and want to take on retirement with a vengeance. They are determined to live an active retirement and want to make sure their money is positioned to support an active lifestyle. They prefer to spend their time living and enjoying life, and not worrying about managing their money on a daily basis. (Pause.) What's interesting is it doesn't matter how they created this wealth, they all come to me with the same three concerns!

"What are those?"

1. *When can I afford to retire and focus on my active lifestyle?*

2. *How do I make sure I never run out of money?*

3. *How can I best continue to support my family and personal interests?*

"So, what do you do for them?"

- *I develop their Active Lifestyle Plan,*

- *I incorporate a Three-Bucket Investment Strategy,*

- *And I engage them in my Total Infusion Program.*

In both of these examples, the three solutions are written in terms that could be labels on a box. That is exactly how I want you to think of this. It's time to package your services with a bit of personality! Most financial advisors have been walking around with their products, services and value wrapped in a tired old brown bag. When someone asks them what they do, they fumble around in their bag, hunting for the right product or service to present. It's certainly not the best way to present a confident and professional image.

But what would happen if, instead of presenting an old brown bag, you pulled out three classy boxes, like those beautiful blue Tiffany's boxes, and each one was a carefully labeled product? *Taa-daaa!*

Think these boxes might evoke a stronger reaction than an old brown bag? Of course! When your solutions have brand names, people feel compelled to ask questions to find out what those packages include.

Going home!

Now it's time to take this introductory script to the next level. You will need both a short version and a long version of your compelling introductory script. The short version is what you have just been working on, where you provide brief answers that require further explanation. In the previous example, the three solutions were:

1. An Active Lifestyle Plan;

2. A Three-Bucket Strategy;

3. And a Total Infusion Program.

No one really knows what each of those programs is. For most advisors, the first inclination is to explain them. DON'T DO THAT! (At least not yet.)

With your introductory script, *you want people to ask for more information* to satisfy their curiosity. This is almost like playing hard to get; don't give them everything they want.

Once you get through your script, then you can say, "Why don't we get together next week and I can tell you more about what I do, and I can learn more about you?"

The long version of your introductory script belongs on your website. It makes an excellent home page. It is clear, concise, and attractive to your tribal market, and it gives people a taste of what you do without educating, lecturing or boring them.

Let's go back to Dan, who manages passionate wealth. Here is Dan's short version, which he uses at networking events and group sporting events:

"So Dan, what do you do?"

I manage passionate wealth.

"What do you mean by that?"

Most of my clients are successful professionals and passionate outdoor enthusiasts. They have worked hard and saved well, and want to take on retirement with a vengeance. They are determined to live an active retirement and want to make sure their money is positioned to support an active lifestyle. They prefer to spend their time living and enjoying life, and not worrying about managing their money on a daily basis. (Pause.) What's interesting is it doesn't matter how they created this wealth, they all come to me with the same three concerns!

"What are those?"

1. *When can I afford to retire and focus on my active lifestyle?*

2. *How do I make sure I never run out of money?*

3. *How can I best continue to support my family and personal interests?*

"So, what do you do for them?"

- *I develop their Active Lifestyle Plan,*

- *I incorporate a Three-Bucket Investment Strategy,*

- *And I engage them in my Total Infusion Program.*

Using his compelling introductory script as the base, he then developed a home page that is short, powerful and engaging:

Dan Jones

A Purpose-Driven Wealth Advisor

"Taking on Retirement with a Vengeance!"

Dan Jones is a wealth advisor and outdoor enthusiast, committed to helping his clients use their hard-earned wealth to live an active and fulfilling life in retirement. Most of Dan's clients are successful professionals who share his enthusiasm for outdoor activities. They have worked hard and saved well, and want to take on retirement with a vengeance.

Dan's client are determined to live an active retirement and want to make sure their money is positioned to support their active lifestyle. They prefer to spend their time living and enjoying life, not worrying about managing their money on a daily basis.

It doesn't seem to matter how Dan's clients created their wealth, they typically share the same three concerns:

- *When can I afford to retire and support my active lifestyle?*

- *How do I make sure I never run out of money?*

- *How can I best continue to support my family and personal interests?*

As your wealth advisor, Dan will help you:

1. *Develop your **Active Lifestyle Plan,** giving you confidence in your ability to continue enjoying your activities and interests.*

2. *Design your **Bucket Investment Strategy,** ensuring your current and long-term income needs.*

3. *Engage in Dan's **Total Infusion Program,** providing clarity, education, active events and purpose-driven communication.*

In the Solutions section, we expanded his verbiage to create a more complete message. He didn't explain what the solution was; he just mentioned the benefits of each solution.

Remember: prospects and clients are looking for WIIFM: *What's in it for me?* Or, *How will this make my life better, easier, less stressful?*

Let's look at this one more time, but this time, pay close attention to the highlighted sections. That's where the WIIFM is.

*Develop your **Active Lifestyle Plan,** <u>giving you confidence in your ability to enjoy your activities and interests.</u>*

*Design your **Bucket Investment Strategy,** <u>providing greater comfort and consistency.</u>*

*Engage in Dan's **Total Infusion Program,** <u>providing clarity, education, active events and purpose-driven communication.</u>*

Christina also converted her compelling introductory script into a powerful home page. Notice how she added more content and benefits to her three solutions.

Christina Advisor

"Wealth Stewardship with Integrity"

Most of our clients are families of faith; they have accumulated substantial assets and are compelled to be good stewards of their wealth. For most, this means ensuring their lifestyle, enhancing their family's sense of safety, and contributing to their community. Maintaining that faith-based balance can be challenging at times. It's easy to lose your focus with the constant pressures and pace of life. Working with an advisor who shares your beliefs and principles is a critical component in your pursuit of successful stewardship.

Most of our clients come to us through personal referrals. They often share the same three concerns:

1. *How can I maintain my lifestyle and not outlive my money?*

2. *How can I use my wealth to enrich my life and those of others?*

3. *Who can we work with that will support and encourage our priorities?*

After working with our team, our clients have:

1. **A lifestyle priority plan** *that aligns their values with their financial opportunities.*

2. ***A balanced investment strategy*** *that incorporates both their personal and charitable goals.*

3. ***A values-based education*** *that reinforces the principles of stewardship and enhances purpose-driven communication.*

Now, it's your turn to get crystal clear as to who your tribal market is and what is important to them. The following worksheet will help you refine your thoughts and message. After clarifying your tribal market and its key concerns, then you can begin crafting your unique introductory script. When creating your script, be sure to follow the flow and structure; it is strategically designed to create the intrigue you are looking for.

Defining Your Tribal Market

My tribal market is:

(Be as specific as possible – who they are, where they are and what they do.)

_____

_____

_____

To connect with a particular tribal market, you must be able to identify with the people and show that you understand them and their situation. In the workspace below, identify a few Hot Buttons – one or two words that represent common needs or concerns.

	Greatest Concerns/Needs (not limited to financial concerns)	Hot Buttons
1.		
2.		
3.		

Based on these needs and concerns, what do you provide in your process that would satisfy their needs and concerns?

Need/Concern	Solutions

INTRODUCTORY SCRIPT WORKSHEET

"So, what do you do?"

Title: Describe your title using words that you have incorporated into your introductory script.

I am a:

_____

"What do you mean by that?"

Most of my clients are (define and compliment):

_____

_____

_____

Define their challenges:

_____

_____

_____

What is interesting is that it doesn't matter (how they became my client, their status in life, how they created this wealth) ; **they all share the same three concerns!**

"What are those?"

List their needs as questions:

1. _____?

2. _____?

3. _____?

"So, what do you do for them?"

(List your solutions as brand names.)

1. _____

2. _____

3. _____

Are you feeling hesitant about going public with your script?

If you feel some anxiety about trying your new script, you're certainly not alone. You wouldn't believe how many advisors spend hours and hours refining and perfecting their message – and then turn around and shelve it. It's unbelievable! And yet, it's a sign of how significant this process can feel.

At times, I have practically forced my coaching clients to use their message. "Don't you dare call me next week unless you have memorized and tested your introductory script!" Nine times out of ten, they call the following week, eager to report a new referral or a meaty conversation with a new prospect – a direct result of their new compelling message.

So go ahead and feel the anxiety – it's normal! – but move ahead anyway. When you do, the results will be immediate.

Fulfilling your promises

You now have a personal story that validates why you do what you do, and you have written your introductory script, describing who your tribal market is, creating a greater connection, and compelling others to become your client. You are well-positioned to make a great impression, but now you have to follow through in order to keep the momentum going.

What makes all of this work is you and your commitment to your clients. This means: if you say you are going to do something, you must do it. For example, if I say I provide educational events, I have to make sure I *consistently* make that happen.

Look at your three solutions and list them in a table format. Under each solution, write the activities that represent that solution. Be specific. If you provide educational opportunities, how many do you provide each year? What type? Where, when and how?

Let's go back to Christina and her commitment to wealth stewardship. She incorporated unique questions in her initial profiling process, focusing on faith and personal values. This became a significant part of her profiling process, which emphasized to her potential clients how committed she really was to running a faith-based practice. In addition, she developed a Wealth Stewardship Event Series that further solidified her unique brand.

Dan asked his potential clients to submit their bucket lists before coming in to meet with him. This gave Dan an insider view as to how each client planned to approach retirement. Four times a year, Dan would also host an event featuring a local individual who would discuss recent accomplishments, such as climbing Mt. Everest or biking through France. These things were designed to reinforce his brand and encourage his clients to live an active, healthy life.

Many advisors who focus on the female market talk about helping women become more organized; therefore, in many cases, they provide their clients with a beautiful binder to help them organize their financial affairs. Again, this is brand development.

There are many ways to make subtle or slight changes to your practice to reinforce your marketing message.

- Maybe you send new clients a book that focuses on the interests of your tribal market.

- Perhaps you host events that provide value beyond the financial realm.

- One advisor I know plans an annual cruise, reserving a block of rooms for her tribe. Her clients/prospects pay to attend, and before they make each stop at a port of call, she gives a morning talk about the regional economy and investment opportunities.

You don't have to plan a cruise to make a difference. Even just updating your profile and probing a little deeper into the interests and passions of your clientele can help you turn a generic practice into a purpose-driven one.

As you move forward, everything you do should be driven by a purpose –supporting and enhancing the lives of your tribal market.

CHAPTER 8:

A Purpose-Driven Process

A Purpose-Driven Practice is much more than a compelling marketing message. If you truly adopt this approach, everything you do is in service to an underlying purpose.

A typical advisor calls their clients simply because their name came up on the quarterly call list. In most cases, the conversation is less than fruitful. In fact, it's often a drag on both parties.

But what if, every time you spoke to a client, you facilitated a meaningful conversation around a clearly defined objective? What if, every time you hung up the phone, you had a sense of satisfaction, knowing you had delivered true value to your client? What if you could do this not just with your clients, but also with every prospect, showing them what they are missing with their current advisor?

What if you walked into your office every day, every week, every month, knowing exactly what your focus was and which questions would drive your conversations? What if you had already sent out a series of drip e-mails and event advertisements that reinforced your topic of conversation?

And what if you had a process that ensured you never missed a client, or wondered if important pieces had slipped through the cracks?

If you had a process that did all of this for you, would you be able to capture more of your clients' assets? Would you convert more prospects to clients? Would your clients be impressed with the value you provide and send you more referrals?

That is our goal for this chapter.

Comprehensive, systematic service

The Purpose-Driven Practice concept was born in a flash of realization that hit me when I first left Citigroup and began my independent coaching practice. As my client list of advisors grew, I started to recognize a pattern: most advisors lacked a consistent, effortless way to engage their clients on a regular basis. They really had no rhyme or reason for their actions and seemed to spend their time reacting to clients' needs rather than proactively addressing important financial matters.

As much as they wanted to connect with and serve their clients (and uncover opportunities for more business), they just didn't know how to proceed. Their list of names would pop up on their computer screens and they would scratch their heads, wondering, "What am I going to call them about?" This fueled procrastination and inevitably caused important opportunities to fall through the cracks.

Based on this realization, I created a simple program that guides advisors and their clients through a series of meaningful quarterly conversations. These conversations are suitable for every client, and they make regular, fruitful interactions truly effortless.

As you develop this process and begin to incorporate it into your practice, you will experience its simplicity and will begin to recognize how you can use this same process to expand your prospect list and convert more prospective clients into loyal, productive clients. In addition, it will make your job easier, your work more meaningful and your value more tangible.

While this process was originally designed to help the wealth advisor capture all the assets and provide solutions to total wealth issues, this process can be utilized by any advisor who wants to nurture client relationships, provide more value and generate more referrals. You will recognize ways to leverage it and expand your prospect list, develop stronger relationships with centers of influence, raise additional assets and open more accounts. It really is a simple yet powerful way to advance your business and raise your profile.

An overview of the Purpose-Driven Wealth Process

You select a specific theme for each quarter; this theme becomes the basis of three open-ended questions that address a specific aspect of your theme or wealth management. These questions form the basis for a conversation that engages the client, helps them consider their options and inspires them to take action. By the end of the conversation, you will have a better understanding of the client, and the client will be more aware of your value and options available to help them achieve their financial goals.

It's important to note that questions and conversations are not designed to push a specific product or solution. However, if a particular need becomes apparent in the course of conversation, you will be positioned to capitalize on this opportunity.

Through these quarterly conversations, you will have the chance to reach every client in a more manageable and effective way. As a result, your relationships with clients will grow stronger and more trusting. By the end of each year, clients will feel confident that no stone has been left unturned. With that confidence comes the desire to tell friends, family and associates about your unique process.

For the advisor, this process also doubles as a highly effective prospecting tool, helping to convert prospects into enthusiastic clients.

Think about it: What if you could deliver an entirely new financial advisory process that your prospect had never experienced before?

What if, after six months of reaching out to your prospect, you learned more about them than their previous advisor had learned in five years? And what if, during that time, you helped your prospects learn far more about their financial options than they ever learned from their current advisor?

The Purpose-Driven Wealth Process will position you as an advisor who cares first for the client, providing opportunities to engage in meaningful conversations, address issues proactively, and prevent them from becoming a more serious issue.

The nuts and bolts of this quarterly process

The Purpose-Driven Wealth Process is based on four aspects of wealth management:

1. Asset Management

2. Liabilities Reviews

3. Protective Strategies

4. Legacy Planning

But the important part isn't the specific themes – it's the process. The process that follows is based on what works best for a total wealth advisor, but you can feel free to customize it according to your specific needs. You can select different themes that pertain to your clientele, or you can even cut the process back to two or three themes per year. This is a customizable program that can easily be tweaked to fit whatever makes sense for you.

For the first quarter, let's say you choose to focus on asset management. When we think of assets, we typically think about money, stocks and bonds, but assets can be so much more. Your lifestyle can be an asset; your home, car, business, even your children can be assets. It's important to take a broad view of the term "assets," because this process addresses them on the large scale. This larger perspective leads to a much more beneficial level of support from a wealth advisor.

During the second quarter, you might focus on liabilities. A periodic conversation about liabilities helps us open the eyes of our clients and explore aspects of their lives that they often prefer to ignore. Most people think of liabilities as debts, but liabilities can also include the loss of retirement income or an aging parent; even a wayward child can become a financial liability. Taxes and the economy also fall into the liability arena, as well as health issues and healthcare costs. All of these issues belong in your quarterly conversation.

In the third quarter, it may be time to look at protective strategies: protecting one's livelihood, home, health, business, even a relationship with children. With protective strategies as a theme, you are better able to recognize unique opportunities that may otherwise never be uncovered. Often, the issues we discover have the potential to make the client more vulnerable and the advisor less productive, so these conversations can prove to be critical in the overall success of both parties.

The fourth quarter often addresses legacy: looking forward, preparing and planning for the future, and determining what to leave behind. Legacy planning includes family, charities, taxes, one's purpose in life, and the principles and values a person wants to pass on. It's about trusts, wills and whisper letters. It's about leaving nothing unfinished, and clarifying what a client wants his or her money to do when they pass. Helping clients explore their wishes for the future, and incorporating strategies that address these issues, is a process they typically appreciate very much.

As you can see, these quarterly themes encompass the majority of an individual's financial issues. Taken as a whole, they bring a great level of comfort to clients – and a great degree of organization to the advisor.

Each theme shapes the marketing activities, tasks and conversations for the quarter. From quarterly letters and phone calls, to newsletters, drip e-mails, even seminars and events, the theme determines your focus.

When you know in advance what you will be focusing on, you have time to assemble coordinated materials like articles or interesting statistics that support the theme. When you operate according to themes, it's easy to plan ahead. Your clients will start to notice that your conversations are more meaningful and consistent across various communication channels (calls, e-mails, newsletters and online postings). This contributes to a highly polished and professional image.

Intersecting areas of expertise

You may be thinking, "This all sounds great, but I don't handle all of those issues. I'm not an estate planner; I just sell life insurance." That's okay; you don't have to address all of these issues. Again, you can customize this process to suit your specific business. The goal is to ask thought-provoking questions to uncover and discuss issues that need addressing. Your job is to help your client review their situation, engage them in focused conversation, and then provide options and solutions.

This may mean introducing your client to another professional who is qualified to help in ways that you are not. If you do this, you provide tremendous value, and you help to ensure more continuity and convenience for your client. In fact, this process gives you a valid reason to reach out and develop productive relationships with other centers of influence in your community.

Let's face it: referrals provided by attorneys, CPAs, business consultants and other professionals are a golden ticket. Considering every advisor is looking to develop these relationships, how do you differentiate yourself enough to get their attention and motivate them to give you qualified referrals?

When you present your Purpose-Driven Wealth Process to a COI, you will see their eyes light up. They will recognize that you have a structured process that consistently creates opportunities to address these issues and generate referrals for them. This positions you as a more attractive opportunity, enticing the COI to develop a long-term, mutually beneficial relationship with you.

It's all coming into focus

You may be wondering, "Do I change themes each year?" The answer is no; the overall theme stays the same. However, you do change the focus or emphasis for your quarterly theme each year. After all, you don't want to have the same conversations year after year! Focus on what you believe is a hot topic, or a topic that seems relevant to most investors. For example, in Year One liabilities season, you may focus on the fact that high interest rates are creating a liability. In Year Two liabilities season, you might address how healthcare costs can become a liability to a retirement plan. Same theme, different focus.

The beautiful thing about this process is that you get to write the script. You can focus on anything you want! The goal is for you to establish a defined and purpose-driven process for serving your clients, getting to know them further, and uncovering new business opportunities.

In the process, your clients are going to recognize that you have a clear method for consistently reviewing their life and financial issues. They end the year feeling confident that you have done all you can to protect and grow their wealth. This becomes an enormously significant differentiator for your services in the marketplace.

As you develop this process further, I encourage you to maintain four folders (both physically and electronically), one for each quarterly theme. Whenever you come across an interesting article, book or statistic, drop it into the appropriate folder, to be used at a later date. Over time, you will assemble a specialized library of information that you can tap into as you plan each quarter.

Introducing your purpose-driven process

The first step to implementing your Purpose-Driven Wealth Process is to announce this new program to your clients, prospects, friends, even family members. (Remember: if they are not your prospect, they are your marketing partner.)

This is an impressive program that systematizes the very best that you have to offer, so introduce it accordingly by sending out an introductory letter. Most advisors should do this by mail to make a stronger impression, but some advisors choose to use both mail and e-mail, depending on the tribal market. Be sure your letter explains what the process is, how it works and why you feel it is so important. Here is a sample.

Purpose-Driven Wealth Process

Sample Introductory Letter

Date

\<Address\>
\<Address\>
\<Address\>

\<Dear Mr/Mrs.\>

Over the past few years, the volatility in the stock market has illustrated the importance of more comprehensive approach to managing wealth. This evolution combined with my strong desire to continue to improve my service to you has prompted me to re-evaluate and redesign my business process to better serve your needs for years to come.

With that in mind, I have developed my new *Purpose Driven Process* focused on the four quarters of the year. For each quarter, we will address one of the following themes:

- **Asset Management** – We will review your wealth objectives and re-evaluate our investment strategies in order to realize your goals.

- **Liability Management** – We will review your liabilities and consider alternative opportunities to consolidate and reduce debt.

- **Wealth Protection** – The focus for this quarter is to re-evaluate the steps you have taken to protect your estate from unforeseen events.

- **Legacy Planning** – The focus of this quarter will be on strategies designed to assist you in the transfer of wealth, family philanthropy, and/or foundations.

Through purposeful and meaningful conversations this process should help prevent procrastination, create a disciplined approach to investing and it will allow you to rest easy knowing that every aspect of your financial life should be covered and addressed. I am excited about these changes and look forward to serving you more comprehensively and professionally.

Warmest regards,

Financial Advisor

It's rare that I ever encourage people to copy a letter or script verbatim, but with this introductory letter, I give you my full permission to plagiarize it. Many advisors have used this letter just as it is. If you want to make some edits, or change the themes and details, no problem.

Along with this letter, send a Purpose-Driven Wealth diagram, preferably printed in color on thick paper so it really gets noticed. This diagram is not about showing people everything you can do for them; it's about helping them grasp the quarterly concept and illustrating the basics of the program. Again, here's a sample.

Purpose-Driven Wealth Process

Asset Management	Liability Management	Protective Strategies	Legacy Planning
Goals and Objectives	Mortgages	Life Insurance	Gifting Strategies
Family Changes	Home Equity Lines/Loans	Long Term Care Insurance	Wills and Trusts
Significant Events	Portfolio Equity Lines	Annuities	Powers of Attorney
Asset Allocations	Personal Debt	Disability Strategies	Estate Tax Planning
Growth Strategies	Business Lending	Retirement Planning	Generational Transfers
Income Vehicles			Business Succession Plans

When it comes to the diagram, it's best to start from scratch and create your own. As you construct your version, be sure that the list of products and services under each heading reflects the tools that you utilize. Try and limit the products and tools under each column to a maximum of five; you don't want the list to be a distraction. The focus is the concept, not the details.

Make your diagram colorful, with each theme represented by a different color. When you print out your diagram, choose heavier paper; that lends it more significance. While it's not mandatory, I do encourage you to mail the letter and diagram in an 8x10-inch envelope so it appears more significant. Larger envelopes also allow you to accommodate harder stock or glossy paper. Alternatively, some advisors send glossy postcards with the diagram on the front and their contact information on the back.

Just as you developed your compelling message around the words and ideas that are attractive to your tribal market, you should rename this process to make it your own. For example, many advisors call it a Proactive Wealth Process; others have been more creative, using terms like "The 360-Degree Process" or "The 365-Day Program" to convey a sense of complete and constant support.

Remember, this announcement letter and diagram helps you introduce the Purpose-Driven Wealth Process as a significant part of your practice. You could easily just begin the process without any fanfare, but why deny yourself an opportunity to showcase your value and promote your business?

When a new restaurant opens, they choose to do either a soft opening or a grand opening. With a soft opening, they just open their doors and allow new customers to enter at will. There is no sign or balloons, nor is there any big announcement in the paper. A soft opening allows the restaurant to work out the kinks before going public in a big way. While this may be helpful for restaurants, it is not the best approach for a financial advisor launching a new program. You want to take advantage of every opportunity to highlight your value, services and commitment to constantly improving your practice.

Be sure this letter and diagram goes out to clients, prospects, COI's, even family and friends. Let everyone know about your unique new process, because you never know what or who will bring you the next big referral.

Launching into the quarter

Start every quarter by writing a brief letter to your clients. Include three open-ended questions which will become the fuel for your meaningful conversations.

This mailing should be staggered out to a select number of clients, prospects and acquaintances on a weekly basis. The number of letters you choose to send out each week depends on you, your schedule, the number of clients and prospects on your list, and how many people you can call in the following week. You have 12 weeks to complete all the calls, so you can space them out over three months, or front load your quarter and get them all done early in the quarter.

There are a number of different ways you can approach this process to enhance your business and increase efficiency.

The ABC approach

When implementing the Purpose-Driven Wealth Process, it's really important that your book of clients is segmented according to the quality of the clients. For example:

A Clients = 20%

B Clients = 50%

C Clients = 30%

For most advisors, their A list already receives a lot of attention (although the timing is probably sporadic). In fact, with some advisors, these proactive calls may seem like overkill for the A-list clients – at least until this quarterly routine gets established.

The B book of business includes clients with the potential of being massaged into the A category, but because your contact with these people is so inconsistent, this group of clients offers a lot of potential business. In other words, it represents the highest growth potential. This is the group where you may reap the greatest benefits from this new process.

C clients typically get little to no attention. Some should not even be a client; others may be a hidden goldmine of opportunities.

The Purpose-Driven Wealth Process positions you to stay in touch with all of your clients, but you don't want to overburden and over service those who do not require all of your expertise. With this in mind, there are a few different options as to how you can use the quarterly themes.

Julie was a $700,000 producer with Smith Barney, and a member of a large team that handled corporate stock options for a few large companies. As a result, a large percentage of her book (over 300 households) was C clients. Either they didn't have any more money to invest, or this was just a small piece of their overall net worth. The challenge was filtering out the qualified from the unqualified clients.

In Julie's case, she decided to first roll out the Purpose-Driven Wealth Process with only her C-level clients. She wanted to use this process to develop better relationships with them and then determine who she should keep as clients.

By focusing her energy on her C book of business, Julie was able to capture more assets, provide more value and solutions, increase her revenues, and pare down her book of clients to a more manageable level.

Eventually, after she was able to use the Purpose-Driven Wealth Process to weed out her book of business, she was more prepared to announce it to her complete book of business.

While Julie was focused on her C clients, many advisors start the program by focusing on their B book of clients, as they often are sitting on more assets and opportunities.

Many advisors hesitate to implement this program with their A clients because they feel they are consistently making contact with these high-end clients. But, don't assume that regular conversations are the only value to this process. Remember, a big benefit to implementing the Purpose-Driven Wealth Process into your business is to give your existing clients a reason to share your value with their friends, family and associates. When speaking to others about their financial advisor, they can now say, "Well, my advisor uses this quarterly process that covers every aspect of our financial lives on a regular basis."

Tweaking the process: the Negative Consent letter

One way to make this process more manageable is to incorporate the "negative consent" letter, which puts the onus on the client to take action, not the advisor. Instead of saying, "I will call you in a few days," it says, "if you'd like to discuss these issues further, please feel free to call me." This can dramatically reduce the number of outgoing calls that you are committing yourself to making.

We all know that your level of service should reflect the caliber of the client. A-list clients typically require and deserve more of your time than C-list clients, who may have limited assets and less complicated wealth issues. Therefore, you may be committed to calling both your A and B clients every quarter, but your C clients may not require so many contacts per year. So, many advisors choose to use negative consent letters with their C-list clients. This approach keeps these clients involved with your practice and helps you stay well-positioned in their mind when the time comes to refer a friend or family member to an advisor, while at the same time limiting the amount of time and energy you invest in these modest accounts. This gives you more time to nurture the relationships that have higher needs and larger assets.

The quarterly letters

Your quarterly letter should be mailed out on Thursday, with your phone calls placed the following Monday. At first, your clients may be skeptical, wondering what you plan to propose or present to them. And while some of the calls may result in an opportunity to present a much-needed solution, the primary purpose of the call is to get the clients thinking. You want them to become more aware and gain a broader insight to their needs.

While a meaningful conversation with your client is the ultimate goal, a conversation is not necessarily required for you to reap the benefits of this process. In many cases you can simply leave a message, referencing the letter and asking them to call you back to discuss it further. That alone may not fill the goal of developing more business, but quarter after quarter, these clients become well aware that you have a unique and defined process that you provide for your clients. It is the process and your commitment to the process that makes the difference. Clients will begin to understand your value and share it with others.

The cheat sheet

Before beginning your calls, prepare a cheat sheet. This is a form that you create based on your three quarterly questions, and it's designed to build consistency into the process. This cheat sheet allows you to really peel the onion on these three questions, ensuring that your conversation stays purpose-driven and focused.

A cheat sheet consists of the three open-ended questions, each followed by bullet points that prompt you to gather more detailed information. For example, let's assume that in your third quarter, while focusing on protective strategies, your intent is to determine what kinds of insurance your client has in place. The question on your cheat sheet may look something like this:

What was your original reason for purchasing life insurance, and does it still apply?

- *What is the amount of your policy?*

- *Date purchased and company?*

- *Is that amount still appropriate?*

Another example might look like this:

How might your health become a financial liability on your future and family?

- *If you become disabled at a premature age, who will care for you?*

- *What is your family health history?*

- *What health issues have the potential of becoming a concern?*

- *If you had to go into a full-time care facility, where would the funds come from?*

Be sure you leave room to take notes!

You can also use the quarterly process to glean supplemental or administrative information from your client. For example, one quarter you may be intent upon updating their CPA and attorney contact information. (This can be an addendum to your three questions.) Another time, you might be updating e-mail addresses, or finding out the date of their anniversary, or asking about their favorite vacation. These questions not only add value to your role as a financial advisor, but they also help you develop a more personal and intimate relationship with your clients.

In a team or partner situation, your cheat sheet becomes even more important. The cheat sheet will keep each advisor focused on the same topics of conversation. These sheets should be filed in the client's file so that everyone has a record of which topics were discussed and when. Eventually, there will be no risk of duplication and you will be confident that particular topics were thoroughly covered with each and every client.

SAMPLE QUARTERLY LETTERS AND CHEAT SHEET

Q1 – Asset Management Letter

Dear Mr. /Mrs. Client,

As we start the year, it's important to take a fresh look at what we hope to accomplish – not only in how your investments perform but also in how you manage your life and plan for your future.

Please consider the following three questions:

1. ***What would you consider your greatest accomplishment last year? (This is not limited to financial matters.)***

2. ***What was your most important financial transaction last year?***

3. ***What do you expect to be your greatest financial goal this year?***

I will be calling you in just a few days to discuss these matters with you further.

Warm regards,
Andrew
Advisor

Asset Management Cheat Sheet

Client's Name _____ Date of Call: _____

1. **What would you consider your greatest accomplishment last year? (This is not limited to financial matters.)**

   _____

   _____

   _____

   _____

   - *Where there any significant family events?*

     _____

     _____

   - *Did you accomplish anything on your bucket list?*

     _____

     _____

- *Did you achieve any personal goals (e.g. losing weight, furthering your education)?*

  _____

  _____

2. **What was your most important financial transaction last year?**

   _____

   _____

   _____

   _____

- *Did you purchase a new car, boat, or anything that required a loan?*

  _____

  _____

- *Did you help any of your children financially last year?*

  _____

  _____

- *Did you inherit any money or come into any other windfalls?*

  _____

  _____

3. **What is your greatest financial goal this year?**

_____

_____

_____

_____

- *Is there any major project you were hoping to accomplish (home remodel, new car, vacation home)?*

    _____

    _____

- *Are there any upcoming family events that may require additional monies?*

    _____

    _____

- *What vacations are you planning to take this year?*

    _____

    _____

Bonus question: How many years have you been married, and when is your anniversary?

_____

Actionable items:

_____

_____

List the things you want to accomplish as a result of this conversation. For example:

1. *Send anniversary gift to Mr. and Mrs. Smith.*

2. *Find a great book on vacations in the Netherlands and send to the Smiths for Christmas.*

3. *Send 529-account application for new grandson.*

Q2 – Liabilities Letter

Dear Client,

In today's world of fluctuating interest rates, we must stay constantly aware of what is posing a potential liability to our financial future. With this in mind, please consider the following three questions:

1. **Who in your family poses a potential liability on your financial future?**

2. **How has the new interest rate environment posed a liability to achieving your financial goals?**

3. **What is your most pressing financial concern going forward?**

I will be calling you in just a few days to discuss these questions with you further.

Warm regards,
Andrea
Advisor

Q3 – Protective Strategies Letter

Dear Client,

We spend so much of our lives building and growing wealth, which makes it even more important to be certain we do all we can to protect and preserve not just our wealth but the security of our family's future.

Please consider the following three questions:

1. **What was your original purpose for buying life insurance, and is it still applicable?**

2. **What steps have you taken to ensure your wealth stays in the family?**

3. **What have you done to protect your family in the event of an untimely death or disability?**

I will be calling you in just a few days and look forward to discussing these issues with you further.

Warm regards,
Alex
Advisor

Q4 – Estate Planning Letter

Dear Client,

Knowing your hard work lives on, providing for others, and ensuring a better life for others... these are big motivators for many of my clients. It's important to feel confident that your legacy will live on.

Please consider the following three questions:

1. **What are the three most important principles you would like to leave to your children?**

2. **What steps have you taken to minimize the tax liability on your estate?**

3. **What would your whisper letter say? How would you advise those who inherit your wealth to use it?**

I'll be calling you early next week, and I look forward to discussing these issues with you at that time.

Warm regards,
Alicia
Advisor

It is important to note that the focus of these letters is on the three questions. The introduction simply sets up the letter; don't worry about educating the client as to why this is important.

I encourage you to put a little space between each question on the page, and even bold them, so they stand out demand attention. You want to make sure that, even if they read nothing else on the page, those questions catch their eye.

When you launch your Purpose-Driven Wealth Process, you must do so with a full commitment to stand by it over time. Anything less will damage your credibility. If you say you are going to call in just a few days, you must call in a few days, even if it's just to leave a message. If you delay the call, your future letters will lack sincerity and command less attention from the client.

Again, this is why you stagger the letters out in a controlled fashion. If you become overwhelmed or have too many appointments on your calendar that week, decrease the number of letters that you send.

Making the Call

If the letters went out on Thursday, odds are your clients received them on Saturday. They may or may not have read it by the time you call, but whether they read the letter or not does not in the slightest way affect your call. Come Monday morning, it's time to pick up the phone. Start the call by referring to both the letter and the quarter.

QUARTERLY CALL SCRIPT

*"Hi Mr. Smith, it's Allie Advisor here at _____.
This quarter, we are focusing on managing liabilities, so I sent you a letter last Thursday with a few questions I wanted to discuss with you. Did you receive the letter?*

(Yes) Great.

(No) Well that's okay, I'm sure you'll be seeing it soon.

Do you have a few minutes to talk? I have a few questions I would like to discuss with you. It should only take about 10 minutes.

(Yes) Great

(No) When would be a better time?

Once your client gives you the opening, reiterate what you wrote in the introductory part of your letter. Then shift to your discussion cheat sheet.

If your call goes to voicemail, it's important to leave a message that reaffirms your commitment to the program.

> *"Hello Mr. Smith, it's Allie Advisor at (your firm). I sent you a letter last Thursday with three questions I would like to discuss with you. Please call me when you have about 10 minutes to talk. I look forward to discussing these issues with you as other clients have found this to be a meaningful conversation, so please call me at your convenience."*

If they call you back, awesome! But if you have not heard from them by Thursday, make a follow-up call.

> *"Hello Mr. Smith, I was hoping to reach you this week but it seems that you've been tied up. I sent you a letter last week and wanted to discuss three important questions with you. If you are so inclined, please feel free to call me back at your convenience."*

It's important to note that following up is not about forcing the client to engage in this process. It's about demonstrating your commitment to this process, and to a high standard of service. Just by sending the letter and leaving a message, you get credit for incorporating a purpose-driven process to your practice. You have conveyed the idea that you're looking out for your clients' best interests, managing their wealth, and making their life more secure.

After you've left a second message, you can close the book and move on.

This program is as flexible as you want it to be. If new issues arise and you would like to address them, but they are not necessarily relevant to your current theme, just change the theme. Your clients will not be tracking your system. It's the process that is most important.

If you get really busy and you have to skip a quarter, go for it. Or, perhaps you don't want to skip a quarter but you need to temporarily lighten your load. You can send all of your clients a "negative consent" letter.

You own the process; it doesn't own you. Don't let it consume you. Remember that this process was designed with both you and the client in mind. It should reduce stress and increase efficiency for the advisor, and elevate the value and perceived benefits for the client. Customize it to make it work on both levels.

Prospecting

While I tend to refer to "clients" while talking about the Purpose-Driven Wealth Process, you can apply this methodology far beyond your client base. It can also be highly effective in converting a qualified prospect into a loyal client, because it gives him or her an opportunity to get a "free trial" and experience what it would be like to be your client.

How many times have you signed up for a new program or ordered a product after you were enticed by a two-week free trial? Why do you think marketers offer this free trial? Because they want you to experience the value of the product and recognize how great it is. This opportunity to "take it for a test drive" motivates you to become a paying customer. When you use the Purpose-Driven Wealth Process with your prospects, you are bringing this same strategy to your practice.

In a Purpose-Driven Practice, you should aim to treat every one of your prospects as if they were already a client. This is the only way they will realize the value they are NOT getting from their current advisor, or by managing their assets on their own. Prospective clients only know what they have already experienced elsewhere – and trust me, their experiences with other financial advisors have not always been good. This is because most of those advisors lacked any kind of process that instills a sense of loyalty and value in the client.

When prospective clients have a chance to experience the ongoing value that you provide, they become much more aware of what they have been missing. So your mission is to allow every prospect to experience your value for at least six months (two quarters); at that point, it's a good to time to either encourage the prospect to become your client or re-evaluate whether this target is really worth your time and energy.

In this "make or break" call, it's important to reiterate what they have experienced, what you have learned about them, and why you believe they should become your client. The conversation might go something like this:

> *Mr. Smith, over the past six months we have had some meaningful discussions, reviewing your liabilities and protective strategies. I've learned that you* _____ _____, *and I think you may have learned that my process is different from other advisors because I am more proactive with my clients. I would love to continue working with you as my client. Is there any reason we can't start working together?*

Don't forget your centers of influence

Most advisors recognize the importance of developing reciprocal relationships with COI's (centers of influence), and take the time to initiate a relationship and meet with the COI... but how do you keep your name fresh in that person's mind so they continue to think of you when working with their clients?

I promise you, powerful centers of influence are on everyone's drip list. They get articles from every advisor on the block. So how do you make sure you don't blend in with the crowd?

You share your quarterly process with them. They will sit up and take notice. Because it's such an organized and impactful process, they immediately recognize its value. In fact, they may even think to themselves, "I wish my financial advisor would do business this way."

Most will recognize that at least one of your themes may inspire interest in their practice and what they do. When the reciprocal nature of your business and theirs becomes apparent, then you really have their attention.

So, as you apply your quarterly process to your client base, remember to engage your COI's in the process – but you'll want to do this in a slightly different manner than you do with your clients.

1. At the beginning of each quarter, copy one of your client's quarterly letters (minus the client's contact information, of course). It's important that this is a Xerox copy, so the COI understands that you actually sent this out.

2. Attach a handwritten note from you (not a form letter) on your personalized notepaper. Handwriting this note is absolutely worth the time and effort, especially if you don't have oodles of COI's in your list. (If you have terrible handwriting, or you just don't want to handwrite a note, print it in a script font, in color, to make it look like authentic handwriting.) The note should say something like:

John,

Just wanted you to see what we are focusing on this quarter... which of your clients need to review their life insurance? Please have them contact me.

Regards,
Aaron
Advisor

The purpose of this note is to remind them of your unique quarterly program and give them a way to identify which of their clients may benefit from your help.

Planning and marketing

One of the greatest benefits of the Purpose-Driven Wealth Process is the impact it has on your marketing plan. When you are maximizing the benefits of this quarterly process, you will be:

1. Mailing out quarterly letters to every client and prospect;

2. Dripping out interesting articles on a monthly basis to reinforce your quarterly theme;

3. Facilitating a small, intimate event featuring a guest speaker who will support a certain aspect of the quarterly theme;

4. Possibly utilizing that same speaker to host a free conference call for your clients and prospects;

5. And including your quarterly theme in your newsletter.

That's *a lot* of coordinated marketing activity!

To make this system work for you, start by taking a little time away from your day-to-day business each quarter to plan these initiatives. Once you have your system up and running, the process requires much less time and energy. Here's how it goes:

1. Based on the theme, you choose three open-ended questions and then draft your quarterly letter and cheat sheet.

2. Working with your assistant, you determine your call schedule and decide which clients will get the negative consent letter.

3. Dipping into your thematic folders, you identify three interesting articles that are relevant to your theme, and you schedule them to drip out over the course of three months.

4. Lastly, you consider whether or not you want to host an event or conference call, featuring yourself or a guest presenter, focused on an aspect of your theme that would be of interest to your tribal market.

That's it! That is the extent of your planning. And it will turn your next three months into a value-added marketing machine.

Your assistant should develop a spreadsheet that includes all of your clients and prospects. Also, in many cases, your sales assistant can drive this process, checking in with you on a weekly basis and assessing how many letters to send out each Thursday. This need drives the agenda for weekly meetings with your assistant (which many advisors tend to postpone).

One of the things I really love about this process is that every Monday, the first thing you do is make your Purpose-Driven Wealth calls. This way, you start the week knowing you have accomplished one of the most important aspects of your job: maintaining contact with your clients and delivering value.

By implementing a Purpose-Driven Wealth, you will no longer question your value. You will have more confidence that you are earning your fees, and you will feel less stressed and more organized. Your focus will be clear and streamlined. You will no longer worry about your marketing, and more importantly, you will sleep better and feel better knowing that not one client is slipping through the cracks.

The Purpose-Driven Wealth Process creates a purposeful structure around everything you do, all the while emphasizing your value and promoting your practice.

CHAPTER 9:

Tell Me... Why YOU?

By this point in the book, we've come a long way!

- You have a compelling message that ignites interest and inspires more referrals.

- You have an authentic story that validates why you do this work and quickly instills trust.

- You have a purpose-driven process that is unique in the industry, engages clients in meaningful conversations and systematically addresses their issues.

Yet, you haven't developed your answer to the $25,000,000 question: "Why should I select YOU as my financial advisor?"

What makes a prospect become a client is not the tools or resources you provide; it's not your plan or solutions; it's not even necessarily your advice. It's the combination of everything you have to offer – plus your ability to connect with the prospect.

What prospects really want to know is, "Why do you care about ME? How do I know you're not just saying all this to land me as a client?" You have to be prepared for this question – whether they state it or not.

With a Purpose-Driven Practice, you have developed a business model that is highly attractive, but it may not be enough. More and more often, you have to be able to connect... to really relate to and understand the people you're talking to.

That's where your value statement comes into play.

Your value statement

In Chapter Three, I shared the story about Peg and her team who, after giving a presentation to a $25,000,000 prospect, were asked, "Why should I do business with you?"

Your answer to that one simple question has the power to turn an undecided prospect into a committed, raving fan who not only becomes a client, but also refers you to their entire circle of influence. So, you need to be prepared with a smart, polished, laser-focused answer that will make a precise and powerful impression.

In other words, you need a value statement – a "$25,000,000 answer." In this section, I'm going to tell you how to create that.

A value statement consists of three short paragraphs that highlight the roles you've played in your life and the ways those roles are similar to the experiences of your tribal market. So, you need to identify two roles or areas of your life that align with your tribal market's experience.

- If my tribal market is women, I might focus on my role as a mother or daughter and mention some of the challenges most women experience.

- If my tribal market is business owners, I may share my experience of growing up with parents who were business owners, describing some of the challenges they faced.

- If my tribal market is full of ambitious types, I might talk about being a high achiever.

Mentioning these roles is essential to making a strong connection.

The third paragraph ties these ideas together and emphasizes your value as a financial advisor – which has less to do with the products and services you provide, and more with how you relate to the challenges your clients face. For example, with women, my true value may have more to do with their need to save time, simplify their lives, develop financial confidence and stay accountable.

Each paragraph should be limited to one to two sentences, no more. Let's look at some examples.

If Baby Boomers are your tribal market, you might say something like:

As a fellow Boomer, I understand the numerous responsibilities you face on a daily basis: supporting your children, paying for college, caring for aging parents and balancing careers, all while adding to your nest egg and planning for your own retirement. Doing all of this – and doing it well – can be daunting, even overwhelming.

As a successful professional, I have learned that my time is best spent doing what I do best, and partnering with other professionals that I trust and respect. A good professional relationship can remove the guesswork, improve results and expedite progress, while eliminating the emotional obstacles that often create unnecessary challenges.

Therefore, my true value as your financial advisor is to become a sounding board where you can openly discuss the challenges and issues you are facing, and where you can feel comfortable exploring opportunities and solutions. I can't raise your family, but I can help you reduce your stress, minimize emotions and guide you to a more prosperous future.

In this example, the roles are **fellow Boomer** and **successful professional;** the final paragraph focuses on a value that extends far beyond the products and services you provide.

Here's another example. If you want to target women raised in affluence, you might say:

> *As a woman who was raised in an affluent family, I learned that great wealth can provide freedom and opportunities – and, it can also create additional stress and uncertainty. In most cases, women of wealth lack the knowledge and confidence to make important financial decisions on their own. When put in a position to manage this wealth, the responsibility can feel overwhelming.*
>
> *As a professional woman working in a man's world, I have learned that when women experience an environment that is conducive to their style, and work with a professional who can communicate with them more effectively, they naturally become more engaged in the process and more interested in making good financial decisions. This gives them more comfort and reduces unnecessary stress.*
>
> *Therefore, my true value as your financial advisor is to create a supportive environment where you feel comfortable asking questions and gaining more knowledge through ongoing education. By creating more open communication, you will become more engaged in the process and more confident in your ability to make important financial decisions.*

For professionals in the final phase of their careers, you might say:

> *As a seasoned professional,* I understand that you have worked long and hard to get to this phase of your life: retirement. While we always look forward to this stage of life, crossing that bridge from saver to spender can cause a lot of stress and anxiety.

> *As a business owner,* I have learned that when you have a well thought-out plan that addresses all your options, you will feel more comfortable with the future and better positioned to enter this new phase of life with ease and confidence.

> *Therefore, my true value as your financial advisor* is to give you more time to focus on living the life you have earned. By helping you plan out your future, high will reduce your stress and anxiety around financial matters, and you will be able to focus on living a full and rewarding life.

As you can see, the value statement is designed to help you connect with the prospect and gain their commitment to working with you. It has NOTHING to do with your products or services.

This may run contrary to what you've been taught in the past, and it may not go with the flow of what other advisors are doing, but this isn't about fitting in… it's about standing out.

Think of your value statement as a silver bullet. While your "story" is a great way to initiate a new relationship, the value statement helps you secure the final commitment.

Here are a few examples of how you can put it to work for you:

- **In a one-on-one presentation with a potential client,** you can weave it into the end of your presentation, just before asking for a commitment.

- **On a call with a prospect,** you can incorporate it to inspire them to take the next step and meet with you.

- **Any time you are facing a prospect's resistance or procrastination,** your value statement can be a powerful way to conquer inertia and move the process forward.

- **At the end of a seminar,** your value statement can serve as memorable close and a compelling way to encourage participants to meet with you.

- **As a component of your website,** your value statement can turn a lackluster bio into a magnetic and relatable description of what you really have to offer. Many advisors position their value statement above their professional/technical bio – because while your technical bio confirms your ability to perform as a financial advisor, it's your value statement that helps you create a personal connection with your ideal prospects.

That's exactly what happened for Marilyn, an advisor with Smith Barney. She had already crafted her story and added her introductory script to her home page; her final piece of homework was to add the value statement to her bio page. Five days later, I received this e-mail:

Adri,

Last week, immediately following our coaching call, I added my value statement to my bio page. A few days later, I received a call from a woman with over $250,000 in cash.

She said she had been searching the bios of advisors in our firm, and when she came across mine, she knew she had to call me. She told me that what stood out most was that my bio was so much more personal and she could really relate to my message. I had no idea this value statement would have such an impact. Thank you so much!

~ Marilyn Black

A compelling value statement can be your most powerful marketing message, an effective tool to develop interest and connection, and gain a firm commitment from your prospect. Without this one piece, you will leave yourself vulnerable, lacking an effective way to differentiate yourself and tip the scales of success in your favor.

VALUE STATEMENT WORKSHEET

Role #1: _____

Challenges:

_____

_____

_____

_____

Role #2: _____

Challenges:

_____

_____

_____

_____

How you will help them with the specific challenges they face:

_____

_____

_____

_____

_____

VALUE STATEMENT SCRIPT

As a _____ , I **understand**

_____

_____

_____

_____ .

As a _____ , **I realize**

_____

_____

_____ .

Therefore, my true value as your financial professional is:

_____

_____

_____

_____ .

SECTION III:

The Launch

CHAPTER 10:

Spreading the Word

You've come a long way in building a rock-solid foundation for your Purpose Driven practice, a practice destined to attract more clients of both genders.

- You have a gained renewed focus, driven by your tribal market, which will help you create your brand and attract perfectly-suited referrals.

- You developed a compelling introductory script that can be used in a multitude of ways, inviting others to request more information about what you do.

- You crafted your unique, authentic story that will ignite conversations and foster a sense of trust.

- You have a well thought-out Value Statement, which solidifies your connection with potential clients and helps you secure their business.

- And you developed a purpose-driven, quarterly process that turns prospects into clients and existing clients into raving fans (...and captures more assets in the process!).

Now it's time to put all of this work into motion.

But before we start talking about strategies and ideas, there are a few marketing concepts that you must understand if you want to generate the greatest impact from your efforts. So I'm going to give you the most influential marketing concepts I have ever learned – and I've learned a lot of them! You'll want to pay close attention to these principles.

Five marketing principles that can transform your business

1. Change stimulates activity. Change and activity go hand in hand. When you increase your marketing activities, introduce new programs, change your marketing message, develop your website and so on, it tends to stimulate activity with your clients. Think of your business as a field of hard packed dirt. Redesigning your practice is like driving a rototiller, churning up the earth and mixing it with fresh new soil. You're making space for new life to grow. Change and activity can stimulate growth, and that is what you are aiming for in launching this new business model.

2. Stay focused. Advisors love to send out long letters, sharing all the changes happening in their business and educating clients on a number of issues. What a waste of time, money and resources! When a marketing message is too broad or too detailed, you lose the reader. (And they'll avoid your next mailing, too.) If you want your clients and prospects to really absorb the information you are sending, limit yourself to one, two, *maximum* three items per (e-)mailing. Remember, too much information becomes overwhelming – and trust me, *your* sense of "too much" and *your client's* sense of "too much" are not the same! It's much more effective to break your long messages down to smaller chunks and spread them out over time. Instead of rolling out your new message in one letter, create a series of short, attention-grabbing (e-)mailings that actually get noticed and read.

3. Don't assume they know what you do. I'm going to bet that most of your friends and family members really don't have a firm grasp on what you do. And yet, they are your most loyal fans. What a great referral source they could be, if only they knew how to describe you, who to send you, and why! As you launch your Purpose-Driven Practice, assume that NO ONE knows what you do. This way, when you speak about your newly designed practice, *everyone* will gain a much better understanding of who you can help and why they should refer you.

4. Don't do chintzy marketing. Because your marketing message is a true reflection of you and your beliefs, it will hold its value for many years. So make sure that, as you market yourself and your services, you are presented in a way that truly stands out. Be very image conscious! If you feel the urge to hire someone to design a marketing piece that adequately expresses your message, or you want to spend a little extra money to make it look good, I wholeheartedly encourage you to go for it.

5. There are two types of marketing: active or passive.

Active marketing is when others get to see you, feel you or experience you in person. It's when you speak to someone, they meet with you one-on-one, or they attend your seminar or event. Even group conference calls count as active marketing.

Passive marketing occurs when you're speaking from a distance. People don't get to feel, see or hear you; they are just being reminded to think about you. This applies to drip e-mails, advertisements, websites and mailers.

An effective marketing strategy incorporates <u>both</u> passive and active marketing activities.

This program is designed to build results over time, eventually reaching the point where you hardly have to actively market your practice any longer – and when you do, it will feel effortless, even enjoyable. At that point, the leads and referrals just keep rolling in.

While the impact of your marketing strategy will grow over time, you will start to see immediate results the moment you start using your compelling message. People will sit up and listen to what you have to say. Some will ask more questions about what you do, and others will immediately refer you to a friend or family member that needs your help.

After delivering your introduction at a networking event, participants will come up to you and rave about your message. People who have known you forever will say, "I didn't realize you did that!" and centers of influence will immediately start thinking of people they should refer to you.

In the first few months of delivering your new marketing message, you may also notice a renewed sense of passion and energy in your voice, and a new level of commitment in the office. Your confidence will grow and your doubts will shrink. You're going to feel like a whole new professional – a unique, talented, and valuable part of the marketplace.

Choose s course of marketing action that fits with who you are. For example, if the thought of doing something makes your heart thump and you break out in a cold sweat, that's probably not a good choice for you. If you don't like hosting events, then forget about conducting a workshop. If you love to host tele-seminars, make sure you plan one every few months and incorporate that into your brand.

Everything you do must be driven by what works for you and your tribal market. This is your business, your unique message; own it, embrace it and broadcast it far and wide.

CHAPTER 11:

Drip, Drip, Drip... Getting Your Message Out

You have worked so hard to create each piece of this program, so you want your clients and prospects to embrace each piece as well. To achieve this, feed it to them in bite-sized pieces.

The tendency for most financial advisors is to dump it all in one letter. This is a very effective way to dilute your message and deny yourself the true benefit of this process. In other words, don't do that!

Before you begin to publicly announce your new message, add it to your website. As your permanent public face, it must be in full alignment with anything that you send out through e-mails, marketing mailers or in person, because it's critical that you repeat or reflect the same message in every aspect of your business.

You can distribute your message in two ways: mail or e-mail. But you don't have to pick just one; I suggest using both. Some people are more receptive to e-mail while others pay more attention to things that come in tangible envelopes. If you do choose to use e-mail, be sure that your message is crafted in a way that gives it a sense of formality and importance. Often this can be achieved through the use of a header and footer, or heavier paper stock.

Think of these pieces like a formal announcement. You don't send wedding or new job announcements on flimsy letterhead; you print them on thicker paper, in color. Consider using 4x5-inch cards, or 8x11-inch colored paper with a design on it. Think about colored envelopes with handwritten addresses. Maybe you can use a special stamp or sticker to seal it, so recipients know this is from your desk, not the corporate office. Before you mail it, ask yourself, "Will this blend in with the rest of the mail, or will this stand out and actually get opened?" If it wouldn't get opened, you might as well not even send it.

The purpose of doing this formal launch is to make sure that everyone you know – clients, prospects, friends, family, even the sources of all those business cards you have in a pile on your desk – gets an opportunity to learn more about what you do, who you do it for and why you do it.

> **Remember: with these announcements, you are not selling anything. You are just announcing new and positive changes to your practice.**

In your initial launch, send these marketing pieces out in large batches (regardless of whether you are using e-mail or mail). For the initial launch, I suggest sending a new piece every two or three days. The idea is to create a flow that reinforces your message with a bit of repetition. By seeing a new piece every few days, people will connect the dots and start to recognize a pattern in all of your marketing messages. If your series of marketing messages is spaced out too far apart, people will forget about your themes and fail to see the bigger picture behind your mailings.

I suggest you develop three pieces that you will send out, two days apart. I might send my first mailer on Monday, the second on Wednesday, and the third on Friday. Then I would follow up the next week with an invitation of sorts. The goal is to keep people intrigued, wondering what is coming next.

This is not the only time you will use this launch sequence; it can become a very effective part of your prospecting efforts. When you meet someone new at a party, meeting or outing, and you've had a chance to get to know them and collect their business card or contact information, you can put your launch sequence into action the minute you get back to your office. Initiate the "Prospect Launch" series of three marketing pieces while you are in the forefront of their mind. If you wait a few weeks, they will surely have forgotten you.

Remember, you are not asking for anything nor selling anything. You just want to stay top of mind. By sending these marketing pieces, people gain a clear understanding of what you do, who you do it for, and more importantly, WHY you do it.

After completing your launch, add new contacts to your bi-weekly drip process. Or, it might be the perfect time to invite them to lunch. Who knows, they may even ask you more about what you do.

Five steps to making a great impression

The process I am about to show you is a five-step process, but you can change the pieces and modify them any way that works for you; just make sure you deliver at least three marketing pieces in order to create momentum.

Step 1: Your compelling introduction

The first thing everyone needs to know is who your tribal market is. When they have a clear understanding about the kind of person you are determined to help, they are better able and more inspired to send you referrals.

Before you begin sending this first message out, break your contact list into two groups: clients and everyone else. Focusing on your clients first, start with a letter explaining that you have been working on your business and made an important discovery. Then present your full introductory script. Some advisors opt to leave the solutions out of their script, saving this for new clients and prospects only – especially when they have made some major changes to their planning process and investment strategy. But for some, the solutions become a new way of marketing what you have been doing all along. It's your choice; you will know whether you feel comfortable with this or not. Either way, it won't make or break your marketing piece.

When you turn your attention to the "everyone else" part of your list, include your full introductory script, solutions and all. You want everyone to know about the strategies and benefits they would experience if they choose to work with you.

When you create this first piece, have fun with it. Let your personality show through; add some humor or share something personal. These traits make the piece so much more effective, and the recipient becomes more engaged and interested in what you have to say. Read the following example, which worked well for Dan.

SAMPLE CLIENT LAUNCH LETTER

Dear _____,

I hope you spent this summer basking in the warm sun (with sunscreen of course) and relaxing with family. I spent it hard at work, thinking of ways I can add more value to the services I provide for my clients. In a moment of deep reflection, I made an important discovery!

While I have many different types of clients, I found that… (Add in your introductory script here. For example…) *most of my clients are successful professionals and passionate outdoor enthusiasts. They have worked hard and saved well, and they want to take on retirement with a vengeance. They are determined to live an active retirement and want to make sure their money is positioned to support an active lifestyle. They prefer to spend their time living and enjoying life, not worrying about managing their money on a daily basis.*

What's interesting is it doesn't matter how they created their wealth, they all come to me with the same three concerns!

1. *When can I afford to retire and support my active lifestyle?*

2. *How do I make sure I never run out of money?*

3. *How can I best continue to support my family and personal interests?*

(You can remove the next part about your solutions if you feel uncomfortable sending it to clients.)

By working with me, we are able to:

- *Develop an Active Lifestyle Plan,*

- *Incorporate a Three-Bucket Investment Strategy Plan, and*

- *Engage in my Total Infusion Program.*

I am really excited about this new focus and over the next few weeks, I will be sharing more about this and why I am so passionate about what I do.

Best regards,
Dan
Advisor
Title
Phone

As you read through this letter, pay attention to two important points. First, instead of using one or two long paragraphs, the message was broken down into smaller chunks. This makes it more digestible for the reader, who's much more apt to read a short, easy letter than a long, intensive one. (Long letters just feel like so much work, don't they?)

Secondly, don't ask your reader to do anything. There's no selling, no asking for referrals, nothing to follow up on. You are simply sharing a little information. This is an unusual approach, and it makes people wonder. That's a good thing.

With these marketing pieces, you can even shorten your signature, including just the basics: name, title, and phone number. Keep it short, positioned like you are sending a quick note to a colleague, not promoting yourself to a prospect.

Step 2: Your story

After you send the introductory script, explaining that you have made some changes and are feeling even more excited about your practice, people should be crystal clear as to who you are passionate about working with. Now it's time to share WHY you are passionate about helping these people. Not only are you giving them the WHY, but they are learning more about you personally, which helps to build trust more quickly.

Again, as with the previous mailer, you are not asking for anything or selling anything. When you share your story, you will add less text to the beginning, allowing you to incorporate more unique paper, fonts and colors. Here is an example of what you might send.

Why I Care

I will never forget the day I went to visit my grandfather in a nursing home – but it's a day I wish I could forget. I knew my grandfather didn't have a lot of money, just his farm, but I didn't realize how bad things were until I saw the state-run nursing home where he would spend the rest of his days. It was such a depressing place.

After his death, I learned that his farm was worth nearly a million dollars! My parents, who had minimal financial knowledge, never thought to borrow against the farm to provide for my grandfather. If they had met with a financial advisor, they would have learned how to leverage the farm to provide a better life for my grandfather, instead of leaving him destitute.

That's when I decided to become a financial advisor, specializing in helping elderly people use their assets to live the life of their choosing. Each and every one of my clients are a lot like my grandfather, and I do everything I can to help them generate the income they need to maintain their quality of life, and live and die with dignity.

> *Best regards, Allison*
> *Advisor*
> *Title*
> *Phone*

Step 3: True value

This third piece is something that few financial advisors ever think about, much less share. Your value statement is the true connector, helping your audience realize that you get them and can relate to what they are experiencing. As your third marketing message, your value statement needs no explanation; it speaks for itself.

My True Value as Your Financial Advisor

As a woman who was raised in an affluent family, *I have learned that great wealth can provide freedom and opportunities, as well as stress and uncertainty. In most cases, women of wealth lack the knowledge and confidence to make important financial decisions on their own. When put in a position to manage this wealth, the responsibility can feel overwhelming.*

As a professional woman working in a man's world, *I have learned that when women experience an environment that is conducive to their style, and work with a professional who can communicate with them more effectively, they naturally become more engaged in the process and more interested in making good financial decisions. This gives them a lot of comfort and reduces unnecessary stress.*

Therefore, my true value as your financial advisor is to create a supportive environment where you feel comfortable asking questions and gaining more knowledge through ongoing education. By creating more open communication, you will become more engaged in the financial process and more confident in your ability to make decisions.

> *Best regards, Ally*
> *Advisor*
> *Title*
> *Phone*

When something like this arrives in the mailbox, nicely printed on heavy paper, people are not sure what to do with it. Many will toss it, but others may hang on to it a little longer than your typical marketing letter. Because you are not asking for anything, they are better able to absorb your message exactly what you want to accomplish.

Step 4: Extend an invitation

When rolling out your new marketing message to your clients and prospects, I suggest hosting an event and turning your fourth mailer into an invitation. It could even be a fun, entertaining or educational event; it really doesn't matter. But, it gives you an opportunity to get in front of people again, and it gives them an opportunity to learn even more about who you are and what you do.

Think about it: they have been getting your marketing mailers, one after the other, and they may be intrigued with what they have been reading. Now you are sending them an invitation to an event, giving them an opportunity to see you in action. Whether they attend the event or not, you have continued to provide value and opportunities, and created another reason to call them and start a conversation.

Step 5: Making the call

When you make the call to follow up on the invitation, your primary objective is not necessarily to get them to come to the event – it's to create an opportunity to engage them in a conversation. This is your chance to profile them and determine if this is an ideal client, if they fall into your tribal market, if you resonate with them, and whether they have the necessary assets to become a valuable member of your tribe. So don't just focus on an RSVP. Be ready to share why you are hosting this event and why you think they would really enjoy it. If they can't make it, look for an opportunity to probe a little further and gather valuable intelligence that can be used at a later and possibly more appropriate time.

Options

For some advisors, doing a major launch feels a bit too bold. They may not be fully convinced that their message will be received in a positive way. If you can relate, I suggest you consider hosting a "Focus Group Event."

A focus group is a small, intimate gathering, typically held at a nice restaurant for five to seven guests. The guests are selected according to their degree of alignment with your tribal market and their potential to be influential. It's always good to have one or two clients participate, but the rest should be prospects, influential members of your community, or acquaintances that would be willing to market you to others.

The real purpose of the focus group is to create a safe environment where you can present your new message, practice it, and get controlled feedback from the participants. This is a very safe, foolproof way to test your message. Every advisor I have encouraged to conduct a focus group came back to me raving about the event and excited about marketing their new message and business model. In fact, some advisors ask if they can host more than one focus group. Yes! Host as many as you want.

If you are still a bit nervous about rolling out your message on a large scale, then create a few mini-focus groups. Mini-groups are similar to focus groups, but you're meeting with people one-on-one rather than in a group setting. You might first meet with a few supporters, individuals who would love to help and see you succeed, and ask them to lunch so you can share your new message and get their feedback. After just one or two of these meetings, you will have the confidence to start broadcasting your message on a larger scale.

Another option, typically favored by new financial advisors (especially those who used to work in another field), is a personal party at their home to celebrate their new job as a financial advisor. This gives them an opportunity to briefly share their new practice and message with everyone at the event. Make sure the focus remains on having fun, taking only a short break to thank everyone for coming and announce your new career. You will certainly want to mention your focus and passion for a specific tribal market, and encourage everyone to send you referrals, but again, keep these comments brief. Parties are for fun, not promotion.

In every one of these situations, you are building allies: marketing allies. If they need financial help, they now know how you can help them. In the meantime, they can immediately begin marketing you and your value to everyone they know. This is how referrals are generated. They must know what you do and WHY you care before they will be inspired to provide a steady flow of new referrals.

CHAPTER 12:

You are a Magnet

We've come a long way and covered a lot of ground. You've invested a lot of energy to complete the exercises and develop your core marketing messages. You are now focused on a well-defined tribal market, and you have a systematic process to address all of their needs and concerns.

Are you feeling more energetic and optimistic about your business? Are you ready to hit the ground running?

Not yet! You need one more thing to pull it all together and really make this system work... just one thing that will turn your Purpose-Driven Practice into a highly profitable business. It's not another worksheet, and it's not another script or process. It's something you can't quite define – but you can feel it. *Everyone* can feel it. It's a powerful magnet, attracting new prospects and clients to your practice, inspiring more referrals, enhancing your networking, and boosting your ability to deliver amazing value.

What is this "fairy dust?" What is it that turns everything in your practice a few shades brighter, lighter and more fun?

It's YOU! Your passion for what you do and your enthusiasm for your process reveals a sincere desire to help. THAT is what makes this all work.

So many advisors start out with their new script, thinking it's the words and flow of the message that attracts all this newfound attention. In fact, it's what's behind the message that really matters: it's you. When you communicate what you really believe and feel about your business – not just a bunch of words and phrases that could be found in any brochure, but truly authentic and heartfelt words – people respond. They can't help it!

The industry taught us to be buttoned up, serious, professional and boring, so expressing our feelings and beliefs can feel a bit difficult at first. Lean on the scripts I've provided and build your brand one step at a time.

You've made a fundamental shift, from selling and prospecting to sincerely pursuing a mission. Your mission is to tell your story and develop productive new relationships with people who want to do business your way. Your mission is to share your introductory script, inspire further interest, and communicate your true value. In doing so, you will be motivating others to do business with you.

Putting the rubber to the road

It's easy to feel passionate and excited now... but what about tomorrow, a month from now or even a year down the road, when you aren't as enthralled with your new message and business model?

It's easy to let your passion fade and your energy wane. With annoying changes in the industry or firm, compliance headaches and more, frustration and negative energy are always knocking at your door. The next thing you know, you've set aside your Purpose-Driven Practice and fallen back old patterns and traditional methods.

This may be common, but it's certainly not inevitable. The following five-step plan will keep you on track, giving you the structure to implement a purpose-driven and inspired business plan.

1. Memorize it. Memorize your script, story and Value Statement. Print it out and post it around your environment. Repeat it to yourself in the car, at home, at work. Ask your spouse or partner to drill you when you least expect it. It must become automatic and natural. You must know it inside, out and backwards.

2. Hang your message on your wall. Many of my clients have printed their Value Statements and stories on large, poster-size boards, gotten them professionally framed and hung them tastefully on the wall of their office. Not only does this constantly remind them why they are in business, but it validates their commitment to any prospect or client who visits the office.

3. Share it five times a day. Challenge yourself to share your message at least five times every day with prospects or clients. Mix it up, using different pieces at different times. Get really good at weaving your story into conversations, or incorporating the needs of your tribal market into discussions. Use it every day, five times a day, no matter what. You will have it mastered in no time flat.

4. Stay focused. Every day, remind yourself why you do what you do. Read or repeat your story, mission, Value Statement, and/or script every morning before coming to work. It's like reading an affirmation. It will keep you focused, reinforcing your message and belief in doing what you love. You can even record yourself reciting your message and play it back on your way to work. Hear it, believe it and live it.

5. Have the courage to fire a client. Be willing to turn potential clients away or even fire some clients that are not aligned with your tribe. This is not just about cleaning out your book – it's the psychological impact of firing a client. When you fire a client, you are living your principles and standing up for what you believe, and no longer honoring money and revenue as your primary motivators. The sense of relief and the feeling of power that comes with releasing a less-than-ideal client is nothing less than amazing. Often, the positive energy created by this event will attract new opportunities.

Commit to these five steps and you will experience greater energy, drive and enthusiasm. Your Purpose-Driven Practice will infuse every aspect of your life with energy. You will live your message, day by day.

I believe...

I am a firm believer in the Law of Attraction – which reflects universal laws of quantum physics and operates like a magnet, drawing to you the people and experiences that reflect your own state of being. Negative thoughts and feelings draw negative events and experiences to you; positive thoughts and feelings bring positive experiences into your life.

I realize, especially for members of the financial services industry, this sounds "fluffy..." I thought so too, really I did. As financial advisors, we come from a numbers-based industry. We like proof, or at the least some documented historical performance. But when it comes to the Law of Attraction, the only proof comes through direct personal experience.

I could tell a thousand stories of times when I was worrying about my business or bottom line, and then I consciously shifted myself into a state of gratitude, giving thanks for the good fortune of having such wonderful clients and a fabulous schedule. The next thing I knew, a big business opportunity presented itself. Or, I could tell you how many times I worried about my kids, and instead of fretting (circulating negative energy), I would focus my attention on the positive aspects of that child, and next thing you know, their life took a positive turn. I know the Law of Attraction is the real deal, but it's the kind of realization that everyone has to come to for themselves.

To really tap into the Law of Attraction, you can't just say positive sayings – you really have to feel the truth of the statements.

If you feel called to do so, I encourage you to listen to *The Power* by Rhonda Byrnes. Every day I get in my car, I commit to listening to just three minutes of this audio course; next thing I know, 30 minutes have gone by and I feel a renewed sense of optimism about life. These positive messages get embedded in my brain.

At night, I often journal about the things that I am grateful for, or spend time in prayer to share my gratitude with God and the universe. I can't help but feel that these moments are wise investments of my energy.

Mastering the Law of Attraction does not happen overnight; you don't just read a book and *poof* – it happens. It's something you consciously work at, every day, so it's good to incorporate a variety of methods into your life. One of those methods is a Purpose-Driven Practice.

After reading this book, I hope you are convinced that there is a better way to do business as a financial advisor. The Keys to the Ladies Room is not about swinging the gender pendulum all the way to the feminine, it's about incorporating the strengths and talents of both genders, it's about respecting and appreciating the needs of both men and women and understanding what truly drives you as a financial advisor. By combining this knowledge you will create a practice that is more authentic, focused and driven by a deeper purpose which will attract more female clients, create more loyal clients and generate more referrals.

But at the end of the day YOU are the magic that makes your practice unique and attractive to others. It's not your company, your tools or your resources. It is who you are, what you believe and WHY you do what you do that attracts both men and women to become your loyal raving fans.

Your new Purpose Driven practice is the Keys to the Ladies Room and will unlock the door to limitless possibilities and opportunities for success.

I wish you a life filled with purpose, and a passion that drives you to a profitable and productive life.

In support of your success,

Adri Miller-Heckman

Adri Miller-Heckman

ABOUT THE AUTHOR

Adri Miller-Heckman is a consultant and coach to financial advisors, specializing in helping advisors market to and attract the female client. Adri provides one-on-one coaching, group teleconference training programs, developmental workshops and motivational presentations throughout the United States. She is a Senior Executive Financial Services Expert with extensive nationwide experience in business development training, as well as an approved Financial Advisor Coach at Smith Barney, Merrill Lynch, Deutsche Bank, UBS and Bank of America.

Like any good coach to financial advisors, Adri's coaching career was preceded by an extensive and successful career in the field. As a financial advisor, she learned first-hand what it takes to build a thriving and sustainable practice that focuses on the female client. Her success as an advisor earned her the position as a national trainer for Smith Barney, and then Director of National Sales for Women and Co., a division of Citigroup – all while raising three children on her own.

Adri's 25 years of success in the highly-competitive financial services industry was foreshadowed by an aggressive and dedicated athletic career. At 13, she was a member of the youngest volleyball team ever to compete at the national collegiate level. The University of North Carolina awarded her a full athletic scholarship, and in the years that followed, she led her teams to several championships, concluding her college career as the MVP of the Atlantic Coast Conference. After college, she continued to fuel her athletic ambitions by training in an outrigger canoe and paddling across the Molokai channel. The drive and dedication these experiences instilled in her served as a strong foundation for her demanding career in financial services.

Today, Adri is proud of the impact she has made over 25 years in the industry – most notably, her impact on female advisors. Adri has led multiple workshops, addressing the issues that are unique to female advisors, and in March 2010 she launched her annual "Breaking the Mold" event, specifically designed for the female advisor.

Adri's passion for helping women has made her a leading authority on how advisors can market to and serve female clients more effectively.

In addition to training thousands of financial advisors, Adri authored the book *Seminars for the Financial Advisor*, based on her own experience of building a successful practice targeting the female market. She also developed "The Purpose-Driven Wealth Process," a program that systematically addresses total wealth management.

Adri has been a keynote speaker for conferences run by Smith Barney, Citigroup and Merrill Lynch, as well as independent firms such as Montauk Financial and WRP Investments. Her most popular presentations address business development strategies and motivational topics.

Edwards Brothers Malloy
Oxnard, CA USA
September 12, 2013